DONUTS

Praise for the series:

It was only a matter of time before a clever publisher realized that there is an audience for whom *Exile on Main Street* or *Electric Ladyland* are as significant and worthy of study as *The Catcher in the Rye* or *Middlemarch* ... The series ... is freewheeling and eclectic, ranging from minute rock-geek analysis to idiosyncratic personal celebration—*The New York Times Book Review*

Ideal for the rock geek who thinks liner notes just aren't enough—*Rolling Stone*

One of the coolest publishing imprints on the planet—*Bookslut*

These are for the insane collectors out there who appreciate fantastic design, well-executed thinking, and things that make your house look cool. Each volume in this series takes a seminal album and breaks it down in startling minutiae. We love these. We are huge nerds—*Vice*

A brilliant series ... each one a work of real love—*NME* (UK)

Passionate, obsessive, and smart—*Nylon*

Religious tracts for the rock 'n' roll faithful—*Boldtype*

[A] consistently excellent series—*Uncut* (UK)

We ... aren't naive enough to think that we're your only source for reading about music (but if we had our way ... watch out). For those of you who really like to know everything there is to know about an album, you'd do well to check out Continuum's "33 1/3" series of books—*Pitchfork*

For reviews of individual titles in the series, please visit our blog at 333sound.com

and our website at http://www.bloomsbury.com/ musicandso

Follow us on Twi

Like us on Facebook: https://w

For a complete list of books in thi

For more information about the series, please visit our new blog:

www.333sound.com

Where you'll find:

- Author and artist interviews

- Author profiles

- News about the series

- How to submit a proposal to our open call

- Things we find amusing

Donuts

Jordan Ferguson

BLOOMSBURY ACADEMIC
NEW YORK • LONDON • OXFORD • NEW DELHI • SYDNEY

BLOOMSBURY ACADEMIC
Bloomsbury Publishing Inc
1385 Broadway, New York, NY 10018, USA
50 Bedford Square, London, WC1B 3DP, UK
29 Earlsfort Terrace, Dublin 2, Ireland

BLOOMSBURY, BLOOMSBURY ACADEMIC and the Diana logo are trademarks of Bloomsbury Publishing Plc

First published 2014
Reprinted by Bloomsbury Academic 2014 (three times),
2015 (twice), 2016 (twice), 2017, 2018, 2019, 2020 (twice), 2022, 2023

Ferguson, Jordan, 1977- author.
J Dilla's Donuts/Jordan Ferguson.
978-1-62356-183-3 (pbk.)
1. J Dilla, 1974-2006. Donuts. 2. J Dilla, 1974-2006–Criticism and interpretation. 3. Rap (Music)–History and criticism. I. Title.
ML420.J113F47 2014
782.421649092–dc23
2013046268

ISBN: PB: 978-1-6235-6183-3
ePDF: 978-1-6235-6360-8
ePUB: 978-1-6235-6719-4

Series: 33 1/3, volume 93

Typeset by Fakenham Prepress Solutions, Fakenham, Norfolk NR21 8NN
Printed and bound in Great Britain

To find out more about our authors and books visit www.bloomsbury.com and sign up for our newsletters.

Track Listing

1. “Donuts (Outro)” (0:11)
2. “Workinonit” (2:57)
3. “Waves” (1:38)
4. “Light My Fire” (0:35)
5. “The New” (0:49)
6. “Stop” (1:39)
7. “People” (1:24)
8. “The Diff’rence” (1:52)
9. “Mash” (1:31)
10. “Time: The Donut of the Heart” (1:38)
11. “Glazed” (1:21)
12. “Airworks” (1:44)
13. “Lightworks” (1:55)
14. “Stepson of the Clapper” (1:01)
15. “The Twister (Huh, What)” (1:16)
16. “One Eleven” (1:11)
17. “Two Can Win” (1:47)
18. “Don’t Cry” (1:59)
19. “Anti-American Graffiti” (1:53)
20. “Geek Down” (1:19)
21. “Thunder” (0:54)
22. “Gobstopper” (1:05)

23. "One for Ghost" (1:18)
24. "Dilla Says Go" (1:16)
25. "Walkinonit" (1:15)
26. "The Factory" (1:23)
27. "U-Love" (1:00)
28. "Hi." (1:16)
29. "Bye." (1:27)
30. "Last Donut of the Night" (1:39)
31. "Welcome to the Show"(1:12)

Contents

Track Listing v
Acknowledgments viii
Foreword ix

Welcome to the Show 1
The Diff'rence 7
Hi 12
Waves 24
Stop! 38
The Twister (Huh, What) 43
Workinonit 67
Two Can Win 78
Geek Down 83
The New 100
Bye 106

Endnotes 114
Works Cited 127

Acknowledgments

This book owes its existence to David Barker, whose championing of the open submission process for the 33 1/3 series kept the door open long enough for me to stumble through. Special thanks as well to Ally Jane Grossan and Kaitlin Fontana for shepherding the series into a new era of continued success, and for handling my occasional panicked emails with calm and poise.

For their patience, insight, assistance, and, above all, time, thank you to: Jeff Jank, Eothen Alapatt, Freddy Anzures, Khaiam Dar, Jay Hodgson, House Shoes, Linda Hutcheon, Chris Manak, Ronnie Reese, J. Rocc, Joseph Schloss, Les Seaforth, Waajeed, Dean van Nguyen, and R. J. Wheaton.

For general support and sanity maintenance, thank you to Greg Atkinson, Glenn Evans, Melanie Correia, Chris Kozak, Jeff Meloche, the crews at YD 286 and HHK Toronto, the Toronto Public Library, and, my parents, Danny and Kathy Ferguson.

Foreword

I first started working with Dilla in '97. I'd heard about him through a mutual friend, DJ Houseshoes, who worked at a record store in Detroit and had ordered an LP that I produced in 1994 called *Peanut Butter Breaks*. Houseshoes would always tell me about this DJ from Detroit named "Jay Dee" who also made beats. One day, Shoes told me that Jay Dee was now managed by Q-Tip and that he had tracks on the upcoming Tribe Called Quest album. He went on to tell me about remixes Jay Dee did for popular rappers like De La Soul and Busta Rhymes that were done on spec, but got shelved because the labels weren't interested. He asked if I was interested in pressing it up on vinyl and we pressed 1000 copies. I had ties to Japan so we shipped them ALL to Japan.

If you listen to Dilla's early stuff from the mid to late 90s, it was all cohesive. Soulful, stripped down, boom bap. He had a formula down. Filtered basslines with punchy, programmed drums and live Fender Rhodes on top. The "Jay Dee sound." I think part of the reason he developed this formula was to try to avoid relying too heavily on samples because by that time in hip hop, it was too difficult to clear them. Songs based around samples on major labels were getting scrapped left and right due to the legal implications. Madlib's Lootpack and Quasimoto projects, on the other hand, were made on a much smaller budget for a much smaller fan base and thus were more experimental: all over the place musically and chock-full of samples. Those two albums, Lootpack's *Soundpieces* and Quasimoto's *The Unseen*, would never have come out on a major label.

When Madlib and I flew to Detroit in 2001 to work on Dilla's (soon to be shelved) album for MCA, the two super-producing MCs were each at the top of their beat making game, yet each brought something different to the table. Dilla's tracks were done in a pro studio and Dilla himself was a scientist of sonics, whereas Madlib was a self proclaimed "caveman and a beast" who didn't care for separating his tracks in the recording process and his stuff was much looser and thus sounded much less "professional." Yet surprisingly, when they worked together on a full album for the first (and last) time under the name Jaylib, Madlib chose energetic, almost commercial sounding tracks from Dilla to rap over and Dilla chose raw sounding, sloppier ones from Madlib for his easel. After Dilla moved to LA, their production styles seemed to meld into one. And after seeing them as a new crew of sorts, I felt like for the first time, they each had a true collaborator as "genius" as themselves and were collectively on to something bigger and more original than anyone else in hip hop. Unorthodox bohemians. Then Dilla's sickness progressed and his level of output regressed. He was supposed to produce Common's album *Be*, but ended up only producing 2 songs out of 11, with the other 9 produced by Kanye. He spent a year in the hospital.

One day in 2005, he called me to go record shopping and I dropped all my plans that day and picked him up. He gave me a CD to play and the rest was history.

I like to think that *Donuts* was Dilla's quirky, totally creative record specifically made for Stones Throw which expanded upon the blueprint of Madlib's *Beat Konducta Vol 1* EP that I had released as vinyl-only the year before.

To say that *Donuts* is merely Dilla's take on the Madlib sound would be a discredit to the things that make it unique from Madlib productions. The way he used technology to change hip hop makes it feel like the miracle of the pyramids. As a former hip hop beat maker myself, I can't figure out what the fuck he did on some of that record, almost 10 years later, even though technology has now made it easier to do what was then not achievable in music production. And yet it's not cerebral to the point of losing the funk or the soul or human feeling. His use of technology is only to accentuate the emotions of the music, not overpower them. It sounds simple until you hear the original samples that were used. Then you really appreciate Dilla's craft at creating and in general, the art of sampling to make original music.

We were set to release *Donuts* in October of 2005, but we missed the production deadline and the distributor warned us to wait til the following year cuz it would get lost in the Christmas rush competing against records like Destiny's Child and Madonna. This record was never expected to do much of anything but sell to the Stones Throw audience according to everyone in the industry that we pitched it to. I heard things like "instrumental hip hop records don't sell" and I'd respond with, "don't think of this as a traditional instrumental hip hop record. Think of it as more of a DJ Shadow-*Entroducing*." When we missed the deadline to release it in 2005, we decided to push it back all the way to February on his birthday. I originally envisioned Dilla DJing at the release party, but again his health deteriorated. I thought it was a temporary thing so we came up with the idea of J Rocc and I doing a whole night of spinning NOTHING but Dilla music for the record release party and hopefully he'd be better by that time come and watch us, even if he wasn't gonna perform.

By the week of release date, we were not focused on the music or the promotion of the album. We were all focused on his health, which had drastically gotten worse. The release of *Donuts* was our little distraction from dealing with what we didn't want to accept was happening. Dilla was dying. I had no idea it had gotten that bad until his birthday, when his mom arranged for us to come visit him at home. None of us were prepared for what we saw that day. I pulled his mom aside and said "you have to check him back into the hospital" and she told me, "I promised him he wouldn't spend his birthday in a hospital like he had to last year and that's what we're doing." Looking back, I realize the hospital released him to let him spend his final days at home in hospice.

His mom was there for him more than anybody during those final months. She moved from Detroit to LA and spent every minute with him, sleeping in a cot in his hospital room. The love I witnessed from a mother towards her son was something I'd never seen that intensely before. When we finally lost Dilla, everyone's concern switched to Ma Dukes. But she showed strength and adversity more than any of us. She was the rock that held Dilla's family and friends together the day he died, the day of the funeral, and for months after losing him.

Halfway through the book, Jordan asks a question that's been on many a mind: "Would *Donuts* be a classic had Dilla survived?" Songs like "The Factory," "Lightworks," and "The Twister" are great in and of themselves, but take on an even more powerful feeling when you listen in the context of what he was dealing with. They give a sense of unrest and claustrophobia which makes me wonder if it was his way of sharing the chaos and uncertainty he went through faced with death around the corner. And "Last Donut of The Night" and "Don't Cry" are just blatant tear jerkers when listened to with consideration that it was his final days. But even without the circumstances surrounding the creation of the album, it's considered a defining moment in Stones Throw's history for me. I feel that way because I remember the feeling it gave me when I heard the early incarnation of it a year BEFORE he got sick again; BEFORE he went back to the hospital; and BEFORE the world lost him three days after the release of the finished version. I'll never forget what it did for me that day I first popped the rough version of the CD in my car riding with a then relatively healthy Dilla in 2005.

I realize that the majority of people heard it for the first time after he passed away, and for those, there's no way for them to hear it without any consideration of the circumstances surrounding it. I remember the feeling it gave me again in February 2006, a week after he passed away as I drove up the coast of the 101 Freeway from LA to SF to DJ what was supposed to be a release party, but turned into a memorial that we had originally cancelled until Ma Dukes asked us to go through with it. The album sounded so different in those polar opposite contexts, yet in both cases, to me and my circle of friends the album was a work of art. It was an instant classic before it was ever an "official album" and a classic before anybody including Dilla knew that he would get sick again. It was talked about amongst us, heralded and praised or whatever, and more importantly, on repeat in my car and that's always the best test. When he first gave me *Donuts*, Dilla didn't describe to me or explain what it was. It was just given to me to pop in the ride.

—Chris "Peanut Butter Wolf" Manak, March 2015

Raise it up for Ma Dukes.

Caitlin MacKinnon did the work.
Nicole Bryant kept the faith.
Sarah Jacobs saw it through.

Welcome to the Show

The Cedars-Sinai Medical Center makes for an unlikely and unassuming hip-hop landmark. Located in the Fairfax District of Los Angeles, the building is nevertheless a monument on the topography of hip-hop tragedies. In 1994, NWA founder Eric 'Eazy-E' Wright died there from complications brought on by AIDS. Three years later, staff at Cedars-Sinai pronounced Christopher Wallace, the Notorious B.I.G., dead on arrival after suffering four gunshot wounds in a drive-by shooting as he left a party at the nearby Petersen Automotive Museum. Kanye West received reconstructive surgeries following a 2004 auto collision. A year before doctors repaired West's jaw, Anthony Berkeley, known as the rapper Too Poetic and a founding member of the underground supergroup Gravediggaz, succumbed to colon cancer there, addressing his condition on the group's final album. Cedars has been name-checked in lyrics from Tyler the Creator, Slaughterhouse and Kool Keith. But, despite the hospital's role in some of the music's most tragic endings, Cedars-Sinai was also the site of completion for some of the weirdest, most beautiful and influential music the genre has ever seen.

In 2005, 31-year-old rapper/producer James J Dilla Yancey underwent treatment at Cedars-Sinai for complications brought on by a pair of autoimmune disorders: thrombotic thrombocytopenic purpura (TTP), a condition that causes microscopic clots to form in the body's blood vessels; and a form of lupus, which leaves the body unable to distinguish between healthy and damaged tissue. The combination of the two would leave him dead within a year.

Lupus is a monstrous disease, causing the body to essentially become allergic to itself: "Immunologically speaking, it is the opposite of what happens in cancer or AIDS. In lupus, the body overreacts to an unknown stimulus and makes too many antibodies, or proteins directed against body tissue."[1] Coupled with TTP, the pair formed a brutal tag-team of ailments that damaged Dilla's kidneys and left the joints in his hands swollen and stiff, particularly cruel punishments for a man who spent his life flipping through stacks of records and tapping out beats on the pads of a sampler. Intensely private, he played down his condition in the hip-hop press, referring to it as "this lil illness," and that he was in "A-1 health and everything." He chalked it up to malnutrition from eating poorly overseas.[2] Even friends who came to see him in Cedars-Sinai didn't ask too many questions: "I poker faced it," said Michael "House Shoes" Buchanan, who was a longtime friend of Dilla's back in Detroit, where they both grew up. "It was hard as hell."[3] But while the illness debilitated his body, his mind remained sharp, still dreaming up sounds that demanded to be shared with the world.

Fans and followers know the story well: despite his own body holding him hostage, J Dilla refused to go quietly; if he had to go, he was going to make sure he left heads bobbing. With a makeshift recording setup in his hospital room, a stack of records and a laptop, he marshaled every last bit of strength in his weakened frame, forcing his stiffened fingers to create the sounds he heard in his mind. The result: a collection of 31 tracks that would forever change the way beatmakers view their art form, named after a favorite food he could no longer eat.

J Dilla's *Donuts* is not hip-hop music. Not as "hip-hop music," is typically defined and understood. There are no raps, no hooks, no skits, no songs longer than 3 minutes; most clock in at a minute and a half. There are beats, yes; there are scratches and samples too, some of which will be very familiar to hip-hop enthusiasts. But none of the music on the album ever resolves itself; resolution seems to be the last thing desired. Songs careen and crash into each other, starting and stopping without warning, never giving a listener the opportunity to fully enter them; just when you're getting comfortable, as you familiarize yourself with the elements in front of you and align your perspective to the workings of Dilla's mind, he flips it on you. For a man who loved to frequently master and switch musical styles, *Donuts* acts as a document of his career in miniature. The original press release for the album likened it to scanning radio stations in an unfamiliar city, a perfect description if the station's program director were playing half-broken 45s found buried out back of the building. The soulful vocal melodies of The Jacksons, Dionne Warwick and The Isley Brothers are scratched, chopped, pulled and mutated into stunning, indecipherable aural pastiches.

Tempos shift gears without warning; time stretches and morphs, leaving the listener disoriented. The atmosphere can shift from sexy and lush string arrangements to aggressive, obnoxious horn loops and sinister, futurist synths, all within a five-minute span, the only constants the crackly static of a needle in the groove, and the alarm blast of a siren.

James Yancey had been many things by 2005: John Doe, DJ Silk, Jay Dee, Dilla Dawg; a member of 1st Down, Slum Village, The Ummah, The Soulquarians, and Jaylib; the Motor City's neglected son and Los Angeles's conquering hero. His productions for A Tribe Called Quest, The Pharcyde, Common, Busta Rhymes and Janet Jackson had made him legendary among those in the industry and fans paying attention. But major label frustrations and a refusal to take large paydays for work he wasn't passionate about had driven him back underground, working with a trusted crew of MCs and other collaborators, many of whom he came up with in Detroit. His sound was equally mutable: setting aside the syrupy basslines and crispy snares he innovated and perfected throughout the 1990s in favor of the live instrumentation, electro-influence and world sounds of his solo debut *Welcome 2 Detroit*, and the lo-fi grime found on the *Ruff Draft EP* and *Champion Sound*, his collaboration with L.A.-based producer Madlib.

"He was always constantly reinventing himself, on a monthly basis," recalled House Shoes, a DJ who met Dilla at Detroit's Street Corner Music in the mid-90s and became one of his most ardent local supporters. "You know, the batch [of beats] you get this month didn't sound nothing like the batch you got last month, didn't sound nothing like the batch you got the month before that."[4]

As the beats that would eventually form *Donuts* began to circulate, listeners discovered Dilla had opted to go in yet another direction, a synthesis of everything he had done to that point, taking the electro weirdness he'd favored earlier in the decade, combining it with the rare groove sensibilities of his 90s work, blending it with the soul revivalism found in the music of chart-topping producers like Kanye West or Just Blaze, and slicing, chopping and reworking it into a sound singularly his own.

"When I heard all that together in the way he actually wanted it to come out, I was like, *Fuck me, man*. These last couple years has completely flipped music on its head once again," said Eothen "Egon" Alapatt, former General Manager for Stones Throw Records, the Los Angeles-based label that would eventually release *Donuts*. "There's no way anybody's gonna know what to do with this. It was so astronomically different from everything that everybody had tried to do with that source material."[5]

All as Dilla's health continued to decline.

Despite sounding jarring and scattershot, *Donuts* is a deceptively unified album, a work that challenges and confronts expectations, designed to be listened to in its entirety: a rarity in a genre not known for being album-oriented. As Dilla told an interviewer in 2005, in maybe the only public comment he made on the album before his death, "It's just a compilation of the stuff I thought was a little too much for the MCs. That's basically what it is, ya know? Me flipping records that people really don't know how to rap on but they want to rap on."[6]

Donuts was never meant for you. It was never meant for me. It's a private and personal record, a conversation between an artist and his instrument, which just happens to be the history of recorded music. It's the final testament of a man coming to terms with his mortality; a last love letter to his family and the people he cared about. It's clearly a record about death; the evidence found in its rebus of samples, sequencing and song titles leaves little doubt of that.

More puzzling, though, is why a producer continually heralded for his ability to find the best part of a record, to pinpoint the prime cut of a song and loop it into a slice of headknocking perfection, when faced with the end of his life, would produce a final work as beautiful yet intimidating and confrontational as *Donuts*. Dilla never made mistakes; friends and colleagues say he would have a beat assembled in his head before he even turned the sampler on. Nothing was stumbled upon in the studio; frankly, his health didn't allow him the time for, or luxury of, discovery. As a prolific producer and dedicated fan with a voracious appetite for the history and mechanics of the music he loved, he knew the records that went into constructing *Donuts* inside and out. If it's accepted that Dilla made his final work a record about death, the question becomes, why did he make *this* record about death?

The Diff'rence

Despite being historically one of the major centers of black culture in America, hip-hop came late to Detroit. In the mid 70s and early 80s, the sound of Motown wasn't the party grooves of The Sugarhill Gang or Kurtis Blow, but the pulsing synths and thudding 808s of Afrika Bambaataa's Planet Rock, brought to the airwaves by freeform radio legends such as Jeff "The Wizard" Mills and Charles Johnson, professionally known as The Electrifying Mojo.

Mojo's five-hour program on WJLB, "The Mothership Connection," refused to be constrained by what was traditionally considered "black radio." In a typical night, listeners could hear New Order, Prince, The J. Geils Band and Parliament-Funkadelic, often in the same block of songs. His eclectic tastes and bold programming decisions had a lasting influence on listeners, including three teenagers from the suburbs named Juan Atkins, Derrick May and Kevin Saunderson, who would come together to eventually create the genre of techno.

"Mojo really had a lot of impact on music in Detroit. He used to play a lot of German and British imports. The first place I heard Kraftwerk was on his show, in

78 or 79. He'd play anything from the B-52s to Jimi Hendrix to Kraftwerk, Peter Frampton ... all kinds of stuff," said Atkins. "He played all the Parliament and Funkadelic that anybody ever wanted to hear. Those two groups were really big in Detroit at the time. In fact, they were one of the main reasons why disco didn't really grab hold in Detroit in 79. Mojo used to play a lot of funk just to be different from all the other stations that had gone over to disco. When [Funkadelic's 'Not Just] Knee Deep' came out, that just put the last nail in the coffin of disco music."[1]

Across the dial on WDRQ (and eventually snagging Mojo's spot on WJLB after he left the station) The Wizard took Mojo's encyclopedic musical knowledge and turbo-boosted it, his nightly mixes blending records at whirlwind speed across three turntables, usually only for seconds at a time. Mills attributed his innovative style as a reaction to the realities of radio broadcasting.

"Some people might say I mix very fast, from one record to another. That basically came from radio. I had to keep the people's attention for a very short time, because otherwise they'd flip the channel to another station. I would have to keep the pace moving."[2]

Even after the realities of radio consolidation and mandated playlists drove Mills and Mojo from the airwaves by the late 1980s, their influence would be felt for years afterward, creating a culture of dance music in Detroit centered on minimalism, where the DJ, not the MC, was the featured attraction.

This isn't to say rap music was completely absent from Detroit's airwaves during the 1980s. *The Scene*, a popular local dance show that aired at 6:00 p.m.

daily on WGPR-TV, America's first wholly black-owned television station, made a hit of its theme song, "Flamethrower Rap" by Felix and Jarvis, and featured battles between area crews in its "Rap-A-Dance" segments. By the end of the decade, aspiring MCs who grew up watching *The Scene* and listening to "Billy T's Basement Tapes" on WGPR's radio affiliate, brought the tempos down and spoke to their experiences. Artists like Awesome Dre, Kaos & Mystro, Smiley, and Detroit's Most Wanted began to carve out the city's hip-hop identity, reaching an early peak with the success of MC Breed's "Ain't No Future in Your Frontin'." A hybrid of Midwest swagger and traditionally West Coast sample sources ("Funky Worm," by The Ohio Players, and Zapp and Roger's "More Bounce to the Ounce") the success of the single kept his debut album on the Billboard R&B charts for an impressive 52 weeks.[3] Despite the magnitude of his success, though, Detroit still couldn't claim a national breakthrough for itself: Breed was from neighboring Flint, Michigan.

To the eyes of the world, the story coming out of Detroit wasn't hip-hop, it was techno, and within the city limits divisions of taste and class were being drawn. The success of techno overseas and the acclaim for its founding fathers (the "Belleville Three" of Atkins, Saunderson, and May) ensured most club spots were dedicated to the new dance sound of the city, to the exclusion of everything else: "Some flyers from early techno dance events had explicitly banned 'jits,' a derogatory term for undesirable elements from Detroit's black working class youth. Of course, these same supposed undesirables were some of the same youth that turned to hip hop. But at local dance clubs like the famous Music Institute in downtown Detroit ... this classist stance against hip hop culture spilled on to the dance floor: no rap was tolerated."[4]

With the dominance of techno in the Detroit club scene, the city's hip-hop lovers would have to find alternative venues.

No discussion of hip-hop in Detroit during the 1990s happens without a mention of Maurice Malone. Originally a fashion designer who promoted techno and dance parties on the side, Malone moved to New York in 1990 to seek out new markets for his clothing designs and educate himself about the fashion industry. During his time there, he became enamored with that city's flourishing hip-hop scene, and returned to Detroit a year later with a clear mandate: bring the energy and enthusiasm he saw in NY back to the Motor City.

What initially began as a series of rotating events and concerts called the Rhythm Kitchen, centered around a weekly function at Stanley Hong's Mannia Café on East Baltimore Street, eventually expanded into the Hip-Hop Shop, a retail space on West 7 Mile Road. Essentially an outlet to sell Malone's designer jeans and other items, the marquee attractions were the open mic battles that took place on Saturdays between 5:00 and 7:00 p.m. The Saturday battles and the shop as a whole became a mandatory destination for hip-hop heads, a space wholly dedicated to the love and appreciation of the music and the culture, and a place for the city's growing crew of artists to network and collaborate.

Malone built on the success of the Shop and began running events in The Shelter on East Congress Street, located in the basement of St. Andrew's Hall (made famous as the scene of *8 Mile*'s climactic rap battles). The night quickly proved to be such a success it moved to Saturday nights and took over the entire venue as "Three Floors of Fun," giving artists wider exposure to a suburban audience that would come into the city on weekends, thanks in part to the enthusiasm and advocacy of resident DJ House Shoes.

Between the Rhythm Kitchen parties, the battles at The Hip-Hop Shop and the "Three Floors of Fun," at St. Andrew's, by the mid-1990s Detroit had finally built itself a nurturing environment and community for aspiring MCs and producers, including artists such as Phat Kat, Elzhi, Eminem, and Dilla's first group Slum Village.

Hi

James DeWitt Yancey entered the world on February 7, 1974, the first of Beverly and Maureen "Ma Dukes" Yancey's three children. The family, raised in the Conant Gardens neighborhood on Detroit's northeast side, was steeped in music: Beverly was a bassist and vocalist who toured playing halftime shows with the Harlem Globetrotters, Maureen classically trained in opera and jazz vocal.

"Jazz was the music he grew up with and was raised on," said Ma Dukes. "Since he was a couple of months old, he wouldn't go to sleep unless he heard jazz, so my husband had to sing and play for him to go to sleep. It was his lullaby music as a child in his nursery."[1]

Dilla's mother encouraged a love of music and performance throughout her family, scheduling weekly entertainment nights where each member would perform for the others.

"Every Friday night was Family Night, everybody in the household had to perform, entertain each other. It was cheap! You didn't have to pay to entertain. You eat dinner and everyone would go in the living room. I had mics in the living room like people have cocktail tables.

So you just plug in, grab your mic and do your thing. But everyone had to do something."[2]

Dilla's love for music quickly changed from a private, personal appreciation into a DJ's need to spread the gospel of the music they loved with others.

"He started playing records at two years old—he'd spin records in Harmonie Park," said Ma Dukes. "My husband would get off of work and take James to the park, and he'd have his arms full of 45s—his little arms, you know, fit right through the holes. He'd take his 45s and his record player to the park and spin records—adult records, not kiddie records. My husband would take him record shopping so he could play all the new releases."[3]

However, despite a continued passion and talent for music that followed him through childhood and into high school, his parents began to have concerns about his future. When Dilla won admission to Detroit's Davis Aerospace Technical High School, Ma Dukes strongly encouraged him to go, to nurture a natural gift he had for the sciences.

"You don't want your children to grow into something that can't be fulfilled within themselves, and I think that's where the fear came in … I insisted that he go to [Davis]. This was an opportunity of a lifetime; they chose one student from every middle school each year. It was a hard process because [students] graduated with a year of college."[4] Dilla went reluctantly, not wanting to disappoint his mother, though it wasn't long before his primary interest manifested. He was soon spinning records at school parties at least once a month as DJ Silk. Desperate to keep him enrolled at Davis, his mother struck a compromise.

"His counter-action was, 'Well, I'm doing these DJ gigs, you want me to go there, my name is DJ Silk, I should be wearing silk shirts.' So I'm like, 'Okay, I'm going to give you that. You'll have every silk shirt.' He had a rainbow of colors, including pink, which he was not afraid to wear. That drew a lot of attention. He knew who he was so it didn't bother him."[5]

Adding further tension to an already strained situation was Dilla's involvement with local musician Joseph "Amp" Fiddler, a session keyboard player, songwriter and producer who toured with George Clinton's P-Funk All-Stars. Fiddler was a neighborhood success story (the Yanceys lived across the street from the church he attended) who would offer any interested area youth an invitation to visit his home studio and gain experience on his equipment, to learn the mechanics of sampling and production. For the young Dilla, it was too good an offer to resist.

"That's where we bumped heads, because he was supposed to be at school early for lab class, but he was at Amp's all night in the studio … He was supposed to be at school—at a school I wanted him to excel in!"[6]

Amp cut a unique figure throughout the city: tall and lanky with an expansive afro and beatnik beard, often sporting large sunglasses with concaved lenses that covered much of his face, he was a walking symbol to the kids in Conant Gardens that not only could they succeed and be true to themselves, but they could transcend an environment already feeling the realities of growing poverty and the crack epidemic.

"I would say Amp served, in my opinion, he served more as a reference to like, 'You can do this. You can get out of here, you can see the world, you can wear weird-ass boots and still be relevant,'"[7] said Robert "Waajeed" O'Bryant, another onetime Conant Gardens resident and longtime Dilla confidante.

For his part, Dilla made an early impression on his first mentor.

"He was the most respectful, the most gentleman-like kid that I had come into my house because everyone else was wild," said Fiddler. "He was the only one that seemed to have integrity, like, if he said he was coming at three o'clock, he came at three o'clock. And a lot of people don't get that your word is everything and his word [was] bond."[8]

Dilla soon became a fixture at Fiddler's, making his first attempts to transition from spinning other people's beats to making his own, applying the methodology he'd picked up during his years of study at Davis. Even at that early stage in his development, his nascent talent emerged.

"When he first started making beats," recalled Fiddler, "he was just looping, but he had a particular way of doing it. Most people would start on the one of the kick, but he would start on the snare or the hi-hat or some other shit and just fit it into the equation, like a mathematician. I worked with a lot of people coming by and trying to learn the MPC [sampler], trying to learn how to produce, but nobody came like he did. They could do basic shit, but they couldn't do anything exceptional. He had an exceptional ear for putting rhythms together."[9]

Fiddler maintained a relatively hands-off approach with his "students"—they were free to use his equipment, but he wasn't going to hold their hands as they did so.

"Actually, what Amp did, he'd play some stuff out [on the MPC] but he was like, 'I'm not going to show you how to work it. You gotta learn on your own.' He was like, 'Don't use a book,'" Dilla recalled to *Scratch Magazine* in 2006. "[To this] day I never read the books to samplers and all of that, I just try to learn them."[10] His early exposure to this *laissez-faire* approach, free from the prescribed intents and restrictions set by the manufacturers, working without rules, planted the seeds of a philosophy that would guide Dilla throughout his career: with no one telling him what he couldn't do, there were no limits to what he could.

Having established himself as a local DJ and gaining experience by the day at Camp Amp, by his senior year of high school, there weren't enough silk shirts in the world to keep Dilla at Davis Aerospace. He demanded his mother allow him to transfer to the public high school, Pershing Heights: "He put his foot down after that third year and said, 'It's not happening. I don't care what you do to me,'" said Ma Dukes.[11]

It wasn't long before he and the other hip-hop talent in the school began circling each other, primarily R. L. "T3" Altman and Titus "Baatin" Glover. T3 and Baatin were already respected as a duo throughout Pershing's hip-hop circles, when they caught wind of the new kid with skills.

"We heard about J Dilla—which was Jay Dee then—a guy who was really dope on the beats who went to Pershing High School as well," said T3. "At first, we just started out being friends, kind of like that. Then he invited us to his house. When we heard the beats, they were way ahead of their time of what was out hip-hop wise back then."[12]

Intrigued by what he was hearing about his new classmate and impressed by the talent emerging in the area, T3 selected a number of MCs, DJs, and aspiring producers to an event at his grandmother's house.

"I wouldn't call it a competition, but just people showcasing their talent in Detroit," he said.[13]

Impressed by each other's talents, Dilla joined up with T3 and Baatin, as well as Waajeed (who had already worked as a producer with Baatin and who bought beats from Dilla as early as 1992) and Dilla's cousin Que. D as a dancer, forming the crew Senepod, a variation of the word "dopeness," spelled backwards. "We were doing high school stuff—rapping in the lunchroom and vibing. Just basically keeping it moving," said T3.[14] When Waajeed and Que. D focused on solo pursuits, the remaining trio regrouped as Slum Village.

While the group is usually remembered as Dilla, T3 and, Baatin, membership was always a somewhat fluid concept. Waajeed and Que. D were never far, and collaborations were frequent among other members of the Pershing High/Conant Gardens hip-hop community.

"It was always some funny stuff like I was the fifth Beatle or some shit," said Ronnie "Phat Kat" Watts, a frequent collaborator who met Dilla at the Rhythm Kitchen and gave him his first commercial production credit in 1995 as half of the duo 1st Down. "I mean, we was crew, so I guess you could say I was an honorary member."[15]

For Waajeed, the group always represented more than music.

"Slum Village was meant to be a refuge for us not to have to deal with hood shit. We wouldn't have to be concerned with the neighborhood politics. It was our out in terms of artistic expression, and ultimately it was our out to get out of the hood."[16]

Despite the good intentions, T3 and Dilla directed the early career of Slum Village, as Baatin had been lured into the fast money and deadly risks of street life.

"Baatin had started selling drugs," said T3, "and we went to confront him about it. He was like, 'Man, fuck that ... I gotta do what I gotta do.' That's when we started Slum Village. Slum Village started as rebellion against Baatin, to get him to fall back into hip-hop again."[17]

In 1992 the group scored a management deal from local R&B musician R. J. Rice and John Salley, a former Detroit Piston turned actor and game show host. The pair were given free rein in Rice's home studio, allowing them to improve the skills they'd already begun to build at Camp Amp. Baatin quickly returned to the group full time and they began developing the songs that would eventually appear on the group's demo, *Fan-tas-tic Vol. 1.*

Though raw, those early demos still feature signs of the innovation that would come to define them: the lyrical subject matter might never have strayed far from the acquisition of wealth, cars, and women, but they maintained a freestyle flavored, rhythmic, often joyous vocal delivery. They meshed perfectly with Dilla's surprisingly mature and fully realized sonic palettes, playing the warm Fender Rhodes samples and thick basslines against bright, cracking snares. While music typically precedes vocals in hip-hop song craft, T3 and Baatin had an ear for flowing in and out of the grooves of Dilla's accents and melodies in a way that wasn't typically seen from MCs, where lyrical complexity was the order of the day. For Slum, it was all about that swing, and if the words didn't fit, *make* them fit. On the four "Fantastic" interludes that appear throughout the album, the trio's lyrics barely form a complete sentence, relying on "ay-yo"s and teeth sucking to pad out the bars, but lyrical coherence was never the point. Instead, their voices become another percussive instrument: Baatin's rasp, T3's cocksure, nasally tone, and Dilla's smoothed out confidence unite to stick and move throughout the beats with impressive agility.

On "I Don't Know," an early favorite, from *Vol. 1*, the MCs frequently step to the side, allowing their sentences to be finished, commented on or punctuated by the signature shouts and yelps of the Godfather of Soul, using some of hip-hop's foundational materials in unheard-of ways.

"[Dilla] had did it [with] just one verse with a couple of stabs, and he came to my crib where me and Que. D stayed," said T3. "We got in the car and he played it. I was like, 'Ah man, that's dope! You know what we should do? We should all pick James Brown stabs and just make it a whole song,' … We just went through a bunch of James Brown records and we just started picking stuff. I got to pick the stabs, and we just told Dilla where to put the stabs at, and we wrote our rhymes around the stabs … I think we did that the same day he played it for us."[18]

"My recollection was, *this group was on some other shit.* There was nothing—nothing— like that out at the time. Nothing sounded like it, nothing felt like it," recalled American hip-hop producer DJ Spinna. "It was almost like they were groove rappers or something, they were caught up in the moment, caught up in the way the beats made you feel and just flowed with it. Totally letting the music dictate how you flow on the record, and not really caring about normalcy. And it further established Jay's sound and established him as a force to be reckoned with."[19]

Slum Village's music, while influenced by the bangers coming out of New York, built a sound that was distinctly rooted in the aesthetic of the Motor City.

"Detroit is definitely more experimental, more open-minded," Dilla said in 1996. "The hip-hop's more creative than violent, like gangsta rap is. Because it's been influenced by all different kinds of music, not just rap; everything from the house music on *The New Dance Show*,[20] to Electrifying Mojo and The Wizard's mix shows. Growing up, that was what we had."[21]

"I feel like, because he came from Detroit, a lot of the music whether it was techno, the real techno, you know, or ghettotech or whatever, it's music to make you dance … I think he had that background, that's why he put that bounce, that oomph in his music, so you can like, get into it," said DJ Amir, a music historian and rare groove specialist. "[In New York] … it was all about you got your Walkman on in the subway just like mean, ill screwface and shit. It's not like you in the car or a club, or the strip club and chicks are all up in your face, ass wiggling in your face, you need music for that. You need a soundtrack for that, and Dilla provided for that."[22]

For Waajeed, the music Slum made combined the realities of where they were with aspirations for something more.

"I think that Detroit, being in the middle [of the U.S.], we like [A] Tribe [Called Quest] shit, but we like gangsta shit, too. We're from the middle of the fucking hood … After 1984, in terms of crack cocaine flooding our streets, [Conant Gardens] became a fucking war zone. It was really tough at that time, so our sensibilities in music were street. But to some degree, we were kind of hippies, so we identified with the East—Tribe and all that other shit. It's like conscious dudes that pack pistol; that's kind of what it was for us."[23]

As Dilla's work with Slum Village and a tight-knit crew of affiliated acts like Phat Kat, Que. D, and 5 Ela continued to win acclaim, Amp Fiddler recognized a perfect opportunity to help break his one-time protégé on a national stage.

Fiddler was heading out on the 1994 edition of the Lollapalooza tour as part of George Clinton's band. Also on the tour were New York hip-hop icons A Tribe Called Quest, who had claimed their spot among the elite class following the release of their third album *Midnight Marauders*, and Amp was determined to get Dilla's music to Q-Tip, the group's primary beatmaker.

Said Q-Tip, "When we started on the tour, [Amp] came by … and he was like, 'Yo, it's a pleasure meeting you, I got this kid, I really want you to hear him, you gonna love him … I want you to meet him when we get to Detroit.' I was like, 'All right.' We had twelve cities to get to Detroit and each day he would still come and say the same thing to me. So, we finally get there and … I'm on the tour bus and … I remember Dilla had on some glasses and he came on smiling, the first thing I saw was his smile … and he gave me his tape personally."[24]

The initial meeting between the two producers might have been somewhat anticlimactic, but a late night bus ride was about to change not only Dilla's life, but Q-Tip's as well.

On days off from Lollapalooza, Tribe performed shows with longtime friends and colleagues De La Soul. It was leaving one of these shows that Q-Tip popped in the tape that Dilla had given him back in Detroit.

"I had my whole set up in the back of the bus. We're driving off to the next city, and I was listening to it like, *what the fuck is this shit?* It was a Slum Village demo. And then I looked ... to see if anyone was around, cause like, this shit is ill! ... [Dave from De La Soul], he was the first person I played Dilla shit for. I was like, 'Yo, this dude is ill, right?' He's like, 'Uhhh, yeah. Yo, it sounds like your shit but ... Just, *better*.'"[25]

In Dilla's music, Q-Tip saw the familiarity of his own influence and that of his peers, famed producers like Pete Rock, Large Professor, and DJ Premier, but with a less rigid, more organic, more *human* approach.

"The way he had shit [equalized], the way that it was programmed ... it was the most authentic feeling; he was programming it, but it felt live, the swing of it, his time signature[s] ... the way that he had the swing percentages[26] on his beats and shit; like the way he had the music partitioned—he had bass where it needed to be, the kick was where it needed to be, the hi-hat ... he was just clean, you know what I mean? He had an understanding of it that he could manipulate it any way that he wanted to."[27]

Armed with that demo, Q-Tip began playing the music for colleagues and collaborators: the other members of Tribe and De La Soul, the soul singer D'Angelo, California rap crew The Pharcyde; without exception, Dilla's beats were turning heads.

"Slowly but surely I started playing it for people, and I called his house, I was like, 'Yo, man, people gotta hear your shit somehow. We gotta figure something out,'" said Q-Tip.[28] To that end, he invited Dilla to join him in The Ummah, a production collective that also included Tribe's DJ Ali Shaheed Muhammad and former Tony! Toni! Toné! member Raphael Saadiq. With Q-Tip spreading the word and his work catching the ears of everyone who heard it, Dilla was ready to step out into what would be his first golden age.

Waves

Once upon a time, no one knew where hip-hop music came from. Thousands bought the records but, for most, the kicks and claps coming out of their stereos were anonymous, built in service of the true attraction: the MC. The first breakout rap singles featured session players performing original compositions or recreating the disco hits of the day, emulating the loops and breaks popular at the block parties where rap was performed. One of these session players was Larry Smith, a bassist from Queens, New York, and early partner of future Def Jam Records co-founder Russell Simmons.

Smith had played on a few hits for rap superstar Kurtis Blow in the early 1980s, but his partner was losing patience with the prominent aesthetic in the hip-hop of the time, all disco grooves and uptown fashion. Simmons believed rap should reflect the sound and the look of where it came from, and, as work began on a demo for his younger brother Joe and his buddy Darryl, Simmons urged Smith to strip away at his arrangements, making them sparse and beat-driven, with little care for melody.

Smith ended up taking the beat from the single "Action" by his band Orange Krush and programmed it into a drum machine. He called it the "Krush Groove." Joe and Darryl wrote some rhymes about their skills on the mic and the wackness of their competitors, and didn't bother with a hook or chorus. Nothing more than a beat and rhymes, the success of Run-DMC's "Sucker MC's" snatched rap away from the disco and planted it firmly on the block, establishing the percussive focus that would come to define the music.

Following the success of "Sucker MC's" and Run-DMC's other early singles, Smith signed on to produce the sophomore album for Brooklyn crew Whodini after Russell Simmons took over their management. Where Smith's approach in Run-DMC was decidedly minimalist, Whodini were looking for a wider audience, something for the b-boys *and* the clubs, and encouraged Smith to take the pounding drums of "Sucker MC's" and reintegrate the melody and instrumentation of the earlier party records. The resulting album, 1984's *Escape*, earned the group their first gold record and established Smith's diversity as a producer.

Talking with *Rime* magazine in 2003, Dilla cited Larry Smith's drum work as the spark that ignited his interest in beat-making: "When I heard 'Sucker MC's' and [Whodini's] 'Big Mouth', it made me curious to how the beats were made. Those songs were the first time I heard the beats that weren't melodic—just drums. Being someone who was taking drum lessons at the time, that made me real curious. That led me into deejaying, which slowly led to me doing parties and that led me into production."[1]

One aspiring producer who was less enamored with the sounds of the 80s was Marlon "Marley Marl"

Williams, a DJ on radio legend Mr. Magic's Rap Attack show on New York's WBLS.

"In those days, Kurtis Blow was the king as producer ... They started throwing little singing hooks in there, havin' them Linn and DMX drum beats—all that dumb shit soundin' stupid. But I was Magic's DJ, and since [Kurtis] was his man I had to play all these wack records that I hated. I was like, 'Yo, man, I can make better shit than this.'"[2]

Quality is subjective, but Marley did change the face of production forever when he ran a sampler through a drum machine, using it to trigger previously recorded acoustic drum sounds instead of the preloaded electronic instruments.

"I was trying to sample a vocal for a chorus and the snare went in accidentally. And I started playing the snare along with the track and it made it sound better. [It was like], '*Do you know what this means?* We can take any drum sound off of any record, manipulate it, make our own patterns off of it.' And immediately I went and got [The Honey Drippers'] 'Impeach the President.' ... I always noticed that every time I would play "Impeach the President" at a party it was the banger. I probably made like ten records with those drum sounds. In the same week."[3]

It cannot be overstated how much Marley's innovation shattered every previously established rule of hip-hop production. The limitations forced on producers by their equipment were removed and replaced with a freedom restricted only by the creativity of the individual. The entirety of recorded sound became the producers' toolbox, and they attacked and pillaged their record collections, working every classic party-rocking break they could find into their songwriting with a nuance and flexibility they'd never had before. Hip-hop would never sound the same.

Marley was also a canny self-promoter: MC's dropped his name in their lyrics, he made cameo appearances in their videos, he even recorded the occasional introduction or ad-lib in the gravelly high-pitched tone of an old-timey prospector. The strategy worked, and by the late 1980s most rap fans knew that, if they saw Marley's name on the record, it would be worth a listen. Popular singles for members of his "Juice Crew" posse as well as his work with acts like Eric B. & Rakim solidified Marley's track record as a hitmaker, so much so that Cold Chillin' Records offered him a deal to produce a solo album, 1988s *In Control Volume I.* The album featured ten tracks produced by Marley, showcasing new and established members of the Juice Crew, most successfully on the monster posse cut, "The Symphony." *In Control* established the producer as something more than a shadowy figure buried in the credits of a record: he was an artist in his own right, a curator and director able to express his personality through his collaborative choices.

"It was definitely an important thing to have a producer thought of as an artist, especially [in 1988]. Up to that point, the vocalist or MC was the person that an album was about. Positioning me like that on the album was something different for the whole game," said Marley. "I had never thought of doing my own album, but with *In Control* I was one of the first producers to actually step up as an artist."[4]

Following Marley's success with *In Control*, producers began to assert themselves as personalities in front of the mic as well as behind the boards: Q-Tip and Dr. Dre rhymed as well as produced for their respective groups; Gang Starr's DJ Premier used his skills as a turntablist to add his own sonic signature all over their records; Prince Paul, who assisted and directed De La Soul's first three albums, was the honorary fourth man of the group, appearing in, and inventing the concept of album skits, and showing up in early videos as a Rod Serling-like host, offering bizarre philosophical conundrums before the featured attraction started.

As DJs and producers took inspiration from Marley's use of sampling, the first wave of source material began to dry up: how many ways could someone flip "Impeach the President," or the James Brown catalog without it starting to grow stale, creating the same sort of sonic monotony that frustrated Marley enough to try and change the music in the first place? One way to avoid that particular problem was to cast a wider net, moving away from the funk and soul standards DJs might have heard coming out of their parents' stereos, and going more esoteric, digging deeper into jazz, fusion, pop, and rock, never discounting a potential source because it didn't originate in the traditionally sampled genres. Prince Paul and Q-Tip had already started down this road in the late 80s, but it was Mount Vernon, New York's Pete Rock who perfected it.

Pete started as a DJ in high school, building a solid reputation, and caught a break filling in on Marley Marl's WBLS radio show in 1988 when the regular DJ was injured in a car accident. He ended up keeping the job.

"Being close to Marley made me take all my work to a step higher—it brought me to that next level. He brought sampling to the world's attention with the tracks he did, and so many cats followed what he did. I wanted to know, 'Damn, how can *I* make beats like that but also have my own swing and aura to them?' And after a while of doing beats on my own, I made my own identity. But I learned a lot from Marley, and from listening to guys like Larry Smith."[5]

Pete's approach to beats not only incorporated more instruments (primarily horns) into a predominantly drum and bass-driven music, but brought a serious crate-digging aesthetic to his sample selection.

"When I looked at [his] record collection, I was so mad!" said veteran hip-hop A&R man Dante Ross, who signed Pete and his partner CL Smooth to Elektra Records. "Not only did he have every record I had, but he also had every record I *wanted*. It was amazing."[6]

Pete Rock's two albums with CL Smooth (1992's *Mecca and The Soul Brother* and 1994's *The Main Ingredient*) sounded like little that had come before: The drums hit harder, the basslines were funky and filtered, the horns brought added musicality and sophistication to the compositions, and the samples were new and unfamiliar to all but the most dedicated vinyl collectors. They also paid close attention to sequencing, and would often include musical interludes before and after the tracks, usually short loops of jazz and soul records (not unlike what can be heard on *Donuts*). Pete's interludes are a testament to his skill and dedication as a crate digger, a quick flash to remind listeners and competitors that for every hot track on the album, he could have added two more just as easily.

And he could brand himself as well as he could produce: where Marley Marl would drop the occasional ad-lib,

Pete Rock's voice was all over his records, sometimes rapping verses or laying down hooks, but most often operating in the back of the mix, punctuating the work of the MC's, doubling their vocals or responding to a hot line with an "*Aw yeah*" or "*Whoo*," just as a DJ or hype man would during a live performance. His remixes usually opened with a reminder to listeners that they were, in fact, about to hear "Another Pete Rock remix." He seasoned his beats with his voice, removing the dividing glass between the artist and producer, while marketing himself in the process, a uniquely hip-hop technique that's been appropriated ever since by contemporary beatmakers including Timbaland, Diddy, and Pharrell Williams.

Pete Rock's approach to sampling and songwriting had a massive impact on the generation behind him, including Dilla, who often cited Pete as his idol. After hearing Dilla's demo from Q-Tip, Pete hopped a plane to meet the up and comer: "[W]hen he first brought me his beat tape I was floored. I mean absolutely floored like who is this!? To the point that I had bought a ticket to go to Detroit just to meet homie." Upon meeting the source of his inspiration, Dilla told Pete that when he started making beats, "I was trying to be you."[7] House Shoes summed up Pete's influence with trademark candor: "Before I heard Jay, Pete Rock was Jesus Christ."[8]

As sampling became the predominant method of making hip-hop music, an interesting thing started happening: An unspoken code of rules and ethics began to evolve among its practitioners. Not "ethics," inasmuch as whether it's appropriate to take one artist's previously recorded work and reconstruct it into something new (obtaining legal permission, or "clearing," samples being standard procedure by the early 1990s), but *how* those samples should be used: What you could take, how you took it, and it in what ways you could use it and still be respected by your peers. Through years of listening, longtime fans could instinctively pick up these codes based on what they heard in the music, but ethnomusicologist Joseph G. Schloss took pains to outline them in his 2004 book *Making Beats: The Art of Sample Based Hip-Hop*. Based on numerous interviews with producers and DJs, Schloss breaks the rules down to six commandments: No biting, no sampling from anything other than vinyl, no sampling hip-hop records, no sampling from records one respects, no sampling from reissues or complilation albums, and no sampling multiple instruments from the same record.

No "Biting"

While not the cardinal sin it once was, flagrantly copying or appropriating another producer's work (or "biting") is still not looked upon favorably, as it takes the work of another producer who found, sampled and re-arranged ("chopped") the source, and presents it as one's own. The general rule is not to sample a record already used by another producer, but, if one does, put in the appropriate work to make a new sound out of it. Controversies over biting can still flare up, as when Pete Rock took issue with producer B-Side for biting the beat to Pete's best known work, "They Reminisce Over You (T.R.O.Y.)" for Chicago MC Lupe Fiasco's "Around My Way (Freedom

Ain't Free)" in 2011, calling it "fuckery," and "corny," on Twitter.[9]

Vinyl is the only acceptable sample source

In an era of digital, this rule might seem archaic and unreasonable, but its origins are twofold. For one, digging for records is considered by most producers a rite of passage, how up and comers develop their musical knowledge base,[10] regardless of whether they sample records or make, "keyboard beats," with drum machines and synthesizers. But there's also practicality at work: hardware samplers generally have limited storage space for each individual sample (22 seconds each on Akai's MPC 3000, for example). But by sampling a 33 1/3 RPM record at 45 revolutions per minute and then slowing it back down to the original speed, a producer could get around the equipment's limitations and squeeze out more sample time at a lower quality, something a digital format wouldn't allow. Additionally, much of the music people are interested in sampling is never released digitally; it only exists on vinyl copies that have since gone out of print.

Don't sample other hip-hop records

Something as simple as a snare sound on a hip-hop record can be the result of hours of labor spent isolating, sampling, and equalizing the frequencies of the sample to get the desired sound. Sampling from hip-hop records is another example of letting someone else do the work, and can be seen as disrespectful to the producer who did.

Don't sample records you respect

The logic being, if sampling a classic record doesn't improve upon the original, it shouldn't be done, and is usually not a sufficient challenge if it is, they're too easily identifiable by the public. And if it was already dope to begin with, why risk messing it up?

Don't sample from reissues or compilations

A corollary of sorts to the second rule, using reissues of out of print records or compilations (such as the *Ultimate Breaks and Beats* series, which collected numerous songs with notable samples or breakbeats in one place) is considered unethical because, "[s]imply put, compilations are seen as a shortcut. They save the producer much of the effort that was previously necessary to make a beat."[11]

Don't sample more than one element from a record

As with most of these guidelines, taking multiple sounds off of the same record is considered lazy, and limiting: What new elements is the producer adding if he or she takes components that were already designed to fit together? It's far more impressive to take disparate pieces and adjust pitch, tempo, and equalization to *make* them fit together.

These ethical codes, typically self-imposed by members of the production community, would seem to center around two axes: "Is it lazy?" and "Is it creative?"

If it's lazy, or a means of avoiding effort, the rule should be the guide; if breaking the rule results in something new and unexpected, violations can be forgiven.

Few producers seemed to flagrantly violate the established rules of hip-hop production like J Dilla. Those who speak of him often return to not only his almost monastic work ethic, but also the fact that he refused to be limited by anything when it came to how he made his music. Just as he discarded the equipment manuals in Amp Fiddler's basement while he learned to make beats, Dilla cast aside any notions of what was expected of him as a producer if they weren't of any use to him.

"The biggest thing with Jay was there were no rules," said House Shoes. "When it started off he used to look for like a specific line of records but once he broke out of that, that's when the fuckin' shit really got wild."[12]

Bootie Brown, a member of California group The Pharcyde, whose 1995 sophomore album *Labcabincalifornia* gave Dilla some of his first major national exposure, remembered the effect watching Dilla's approach had on him: "Jay Dee didn't have those rules. He sampled from anything, he'd sample something that came out yesterday, CD, cassette tape, it didn't make a difference. And for me to see what the product was after he would do something like that, it kind of erased the boundaries of like, 'man, it's only *me* putting me in this frame of mind of holding myself back, I need to just do whatever I want to do.' That's what music is, experimentation."[13]

Even the most shallow look through Dilla's extensive catalog of beats will show that during his career he seemed to make it a point to return to records and breaks that were staples of hip-hop production, as though he were working through some sort of checklist, to prove that he could take any record and make something listeners hadn't heard before. Using songs like "Footsteps in the Dark" by The Isley Brothers, "Genius of Love" by Tom Tom Club, or Bob James's "Take Me to the Mardi Gras" could be considered biting in some circles, given how frequently they've been used. But the work Dilla put into twisting and chopping his source material into something original could not be denied. As he wrote in the liner notes for his 2001 album *Welcome 2 Detroit*, "I like to 'freak' shit that's been abused, just 2 see if I can do something different with it."[14] No moment typifies this philosophy more than the origins of the song "Little Brother" by Black Star, a favorite anecdote of Roots drummer Questlove, who witnessed parts of its assembly.

It's universally acknowledged that Dilla was always working, always making beats. Sometimes he would make beats he had no intention of ever selling to MCs, he just considered them practice (Waajeed released three volumes of these "practice beats" on his Bling47 label between 2002 and 2005). Occasionally, this practice took the form of finding alternative ways to sample deep cuts already used by other producers. While killing time at Dilla's house waiting for a flight in 1999, Questlove heard Dilla playing around with the Roy Ayers song "Ain't Got No Time," which had been looped by Pete Rock and used as a brief interlude, no small feat considering Ayers sings or speaks throughout most of the song's two and a half minutes. After concluding that there was no obvious loop he could take, Dilla did the only reasonable thing he could think of: he made one.

According to Questlove, "Dilla goes through the entire two minutes and twenty-seven seconds of 'Ain't

Got No Time' and he literally takes one second, or less than one second … half-second pieces, of all the parts of the song that Roy Ayers is not talking … and what he does is, he masterfully places it together and somehow makes it sound fluid. When you play 'Little Brother' for anybody you're just like, 'Oh, okay, it's an eight-bar loop.' But no, he literally took half-second chops, thirty-two times, and made it sound fluid … This was like when Matt Damon saw that math problem in *Good Will Hunting*, this was that."[15]

Questlove pleaded with Dilla to make him a copy of the beat, but he refused, not wanting to be seen as disrespecting his idol. "[H]e was like, 'Naw, man, this is one of Pete's beats, I can't do it.'"

Lifting that Roy Ayers song, under any other circumstance, could have been considered a felonious offense of the beatmaker's ethics, biting at its most flagrant, and Dilla knew it. It was only divine providence that saw fifteen seconds of it accidentally end up on a beat tape passed to Mos Def and Talib Kweli, who looped it straight from the cassette to make "Little Brother," a song that resembles Pete's interlude, but has its own melody and rhythms. Without Dilla's willingness to abandon the conventions of hip-hop production, the song would never have been made. No one else would have had the audacity to try.

"What's interesting about that to me is that the producers I knew at the time still really respected him," said Schloss. "In fact, I remember that a lot of the people I was working with considered him one of their favorite producers when he was still working with Slum Village. I haven't gone back and asked them about it, but my guess would be that they felt that his creativity outweighed any perceived violations."

Even with his refusal to adhere to the "rules" of his craft, Dilla's transgressions never injured his credibility in the production community because they always passed the dual litmus tests of laziness and creativity. One could accuse "Little Brother" of biting Pete Rock, but no one could say that it cut corners, or that the resulting music didn't advance and inspire the artform. He always refused to limit himself, he valued his ears over what the accepted rules of production might dictate he do. He would program his drums ahead of or behind the beat, or lift a sample from any source in any genre from funk and soul to lounge and folk, and still make something wholly his own, a fearlessness that cemented his position among the all time greats of the art form.

As Pete Rock himself said shortly after Dilla's passing, "In the beginning of my career, I did a lot of new things. And this guy took it at least two or three levels higher than me. It was a chain reaction. It was like from Larry Smith to Marley Marl, Marley Marl to Pete Rock, from Pete Rock to Jay Dee."[16]

Stop!

J Dilla would hate this book.

I'll never know this for a fact, and he'll never be able to tell me himself, but everything I've read, everything I know about the man suggests he would not be a fan. This sort of intense examination of his older work seemed to make him extremely uncomfortable. His focus was always on forward movement.

Frank Nitt, half of Detroit rap duo Frank-n-Dank and one of Dilla's oldest friends, told a documentary crew in 2010, "I know that for him, he was always on to the next. He kind of let it all go at some point. I think what bothered him the most [was] people would call him about something he did three months ago. And he'd be like *Aw, man, they want this old-ass beat, I don't even want to fuck with this beat right now, it's old to me*."[1]

House Shoes concurred: "[He'd] get on one page, he would conquer that and be satisfied and then he would move on … and he wouldn't look back, there was always no looking back with Jay. Like, 'I did that, I'm done with it, let's go five years ahead.'"[2] If Dilla's career is any indication, the music he might have made after *Donuts* would certainly have sounded markedly different from anything he did before. In a musical landscape filled with trap beats, electro and dubstep, I could try to predict what sounds might have caught his attention and inspired him. But he's not here, so I'll never know.

This leads to a common rebuttal to those who would claim the album's greatness: Would *Donuts* be considered a classic had Dilla survived? Would we still be talking about it? Would it still possess the haunted power that it does? Would I be writing this book? Or would it just be some anomalous blip in his discography, an artifact left over from a bout of bad health? Maybe it would. But I'll never know.

There are a lot of things I won't know. Regardless of what myths and rumors swirl around the album's creation, despite how personally many fans might cherish it, *Donuts* is the singular vision of James Yancey, with very little collaboration from anyone else. No matter what evidence can be pulled from the album, no matter how sound my arguments or anyone else's might seem, the purest truth is that no one knows what Dilla was thinking when he selected those samples and manipulated them in the ways that he did. A non-lexical chant sampled on the song "People" is taken from "Mujhe Maar Daalo," a track from the 1974 Hindi movie *Geeta Mera Naam*. The actual lyrics of the song, when translated to English, tell the story of a woman facing her demise, seeking to prove that life does not end with death. Is it even in the realm of possibility that Dilla knew that when he decided to sample that song? Only he knew. Whether the point was to make a grand statement on the nature of mortality, or assert how dominant his beatmaking skills were, no one can say definitively what he intended. Any inference

I make regarding those intentions is, in a way, speaking for Dilla, and that's a proposition I find more than a little discomfiting.

But isn't that, to some extent, the entire purpose of criticism? To pull meaning and appreciation from a work of art through the prism of one's experience, as well as an understanding of its historical and biographical context and one's familiarity with the conventions of the genre?

The predominant tension among critics of the last 80 years revolves around these ideas of authorial intention: Essentially, whose opinion matters more, the person who produces the work or the person who consumes it? For most of the twentieth century, multiple schools of thought, including the so-called "New Criticism," post-structuralism, and deconstructivism argued that meaning should be derived only from what can be extracted from the work itself through close reading; that is what matters, the artist is little more than what the poet T. S. Eliot considered a "medium," free of personality. Or, as the critics W. K. Wimsatt and Monroe Beardsley posit in their essay "The Intentional Fallacy": "The poem is not the critic's own and not the author's (it is detached from the author at birth and goes about the world beyond his power to intend about it or control it). The poem belongs to the public." Wimsatt and Beardsley might have been discussing poetry, but the idea is equally applicable to any work of art, including *Donuts*. By this reasoning, the inability to know or verify what Dilla meant makes no difference to what I might take away from repeated listens, because what he might have been thinking or feeling when he made it is irrelevant to my interpretation.

But.

The formalist sensibility only works if I can commit to it fully, and, if I do, I end up thinking my way into a paradox: What Dilla might have thought or felt as he made the album is irrelevant to the meaning I pull out of it, but what if the meaning I pull out has *everything* to do with what I think Dilla might have thought or felt? This line of thought also demands not only that all evidence be contained in the object, but that the object exists free of any other historical or cultural influence, and that's something I can't do. One man created *Donuts*, but it didn't spring forth from a vacuum. It's the product of a cultural tradition, and the end point of decade-long career; I can't ignore these factors. What I'm trying to do probably ends up falling more in line with the historicist, reader-response schools, where interpretation is a collaborative process between the artist and the listener: I extract meaning from the album based on what I know, while acknowledging what was going on at the time, both in his life and the larger musical landscape.

Ultimately, my mind is too feeble to deem one path "correct"; I'm just trying to establish the precedent at work here. The truth is, there are many people who don't think *Donuts* has anything to do with dying; they just let the album breathe as it is. I happen to think it's very much about mortality, in more ways than Dilla might have even realized. And my opinion isn't any "more right" than theirs; "rightness" isn't the point here. The point is that when any album enters the public space, the creators of the work relinquish their right to dictate what the listener takes away from it.

"*Donuts* has proven itself as a great work of art [because it's] open to theories like that—this is great," said Jeff Jank, longtime Art Director at Stones Throw Records, who worked closely with Dilla on the album as it moved to completion.

"Dilla went from being his own person with a lot of privacy, to being the public's person. The public discussion about the work has become a part of it."[3]

There might be many things I'll never know about this record, but that doesn't mean the questions shouldn't be asked.

The Twister (Huh, What)

By 2003 J Dilla had established himself as one of the best producers in the industry, and had built a catalog impressive by any standard. He'd provided classic tracks for The Pharcyde, De La Soul, and Busta Rhymes. He'd co-produced the last two A Tribe Called Quest albums, *Beats, Rhymes and Life* in 1996, followed by *The Love Movement* in 1998. The year 2000 was particularly good to him: As part of a loose collection of likeminded artists called "The Soulquarians," he manned the boards for most of Common's critical and commercial breakthrough *Like Water for Chocolate*, inspired the musical aesthetic of D'Angelo's album *Voodoo*, and released Slum Village's sophomore album, *Fantastic Volume 2*.

Originally recorded in 1998, *Volume 2* delivered on the promise of its predecessor, offering a mix of rerecorded tracks from the initial demos as well as new material. For many fans of his work, that album was their first uncut glimpse into what Dilla was capable of when he made music for himself, and proof that he'd perfected the sloppy drums, soupy bass, and chopped-up keyboards that typified his sound during that period in his career.

"Eighty to ninety percent of all these joints that people have heard? Fifteen minutes, twenty minutes tops. The first beat I ever saw him make was 'Get a Hold,' off of *Beats, Rhymes and Life* … and it probably took him about twelve minutes to make. And he was getting frustrated. He was getting frustrated on the drums. Finally he got them, and then just to chop the loop up and put it on top took him like two, three minutes," said House Shoes.[1]

Dilla's increasing success, combined with a ravenous fan base constantly hungering for new material, meant that, by the time *Volume 2* was released, it had already leaked and been heavily bootlegged, though that never seemed to bother Dilla very much.

"They say we went multiplatinum in the streets because it was bootlegged, I mean everybody at different companies bootlegged to the point that when it finally came out, everybody already had it," he told the BBC in 2001, "But it's all good. I thank the bootleggers because you actually helped me. That gave me a little, I guess you would say power in this industry … It took all of that bootlegging for the labels to look at it and say, okay, people want this, so let's get on it. So I appreciate everything. It's cool with me."[2]

Due to the heavy delays and piracy, *Volume 2* inadvertently acted as a capstone to the first phase of Dilla's career. "We made that when everything else coming out was real harsh and hardcore. We always tried to do what everybody wasn't doing, so that album was directed towards the females, really," Dilla said in 2003. "We had a couple of songs on there for the DJs and production heads, but the majority of the album was real soft. Then when we came out, finally, that's when everybody else was doing soft shit."[3] With his sound becoming the standard and no longer the outlier, he started getting restless, eager to change his style.

He didn't have to wait long for the chance. The English label Barely Breaking Even offered him the opportunity to kick off their "Beat Generation" series of compilations, designed to give solo opportunities to noteworthy beatmakers and DJs, in the tradition of Marley Marl's *In Control*.[4] The resulting album, 2001's *Welcome 2 Detroit*, the first to feature the "J Dilla" moniker (changed to avoid confusion with Atlanta-based producer Jermaine Dupri, who also went by "JD"), was a watershed moment in his career, and a notice to listeners that he was preparing to broaden his sonic range. As he wrote in the album's liner notes, "Originally I went into this project 2 produce a breakbeat LP. What happened? BBE basically told me to do whatever I wanted to do. UH OH!" *Welcome 2 Detroit* offered listeners the first glimpses into where Dilla was headed, a mix of live instrumentation, world music, and the sort of Kraftwerkian electronic sounds that wouldn't have sounded out of place on The Electrifying Mojo's radio show 20 years earlier. All the buzz paid off when he signed a production deal with MCA Records later that year.

But for all his momentum, Dilla had also witnessed more than his share of industry controversy by 2003. He'd watched The Pharcyde implode in front of his eyes, frequently telling the story of two members getting into an actual fistfight over the merits of competing drum filters. He'd watched Tribe fall apart as well, and left Slum Village as a full-time member not only to focus on his solo career, but also to avoid the same outcome between himself and the people he came up with.

"Sometimes that friction is a lil too much to handle and I was glad that I was able to walk away before ill shit went down like fighting with niggas on some crazy shit. Like I seen from Pharcyde to Tribe to all that shit, you being able to see that shit behind the scenes … I saw that shit about to happen and that's exactly the path that we were on."[5]

T3 recalled, "[W]e were doing a photo shoot. He pulled me aside and he was like, 'Yo, 3, man, I think y'all got this. Y'all can handle this, y'all don't need me for this, man. I've got some other stuff I want to do,' or whatever … I wasn't mad—even though I was kind of mad—but I gotta respect the man who was up front and honest with me."[6]

There was also the matter of the mysterious circumstances surrounding the creation of Janet Jackson's 1997 single "Got Til It's Gone." While production is credited to Jackson and her frequent songwriting partners Jimmy Jam and Terry Lewis, the song features all the hallmarks of Ummah-era J Dilla, from the gurgly bass and keys to the crack of the snare and the Q-Tip rap break, leaving some questions regarding who actually produced the track.

Dilla, for his part, tried to remain diplomatic: "That doesn't sound like a Jimmy Jam and Terry Lewis beat, not to say any names, but it just doesn't sound like it. I know they couldn't have done it. Why is Q-Tip rapping on it, it sounds like a Tribe beat. We all had an input into that, me, Tip and Ali. In this game there's cats coming up producing and have had joints come out and [their] name is not on it. It's all good, it's all good. In the end you just gotta stay focused."[7] Still, when it came time to do the remix, he couldn't help himself. He turned up the low frequencies, filtered the organ, packed on the kick drum notes and made the snare extra dry, all of his trademark maneuvers. He called it the "Ummah Jay Dee's Revenge Mix."

Problems began to develop on the streets as well as in the studio. Dilla was as meticulous about his appearance as his production, and, as record company money started coming in, he wasn't above splurging a little to keep himself looking right. According to Karriem Riggins, a session drummer who met Dilla through Common and played on *Welcome 2 Detroit*, "He was fresh, man. He would always come fresh. I would go shopping with him sometimes and he would go and pick the illest stuff … the crib was crazy, he had racks of clothes, he had a room, it looked like a store."[8]

But Detroit could be a difficult place for a young black man who took pride in his appearance, and Dilla soon found his encounters with the city's police force were increasing dramatically.

"He caught so much flack from the police for being a clean young man," said Ma Dukes, "The police department was down the street from where we lived, and every time he pulled off they'd stop him and harass him. They even tossed the car once looking for something; because he was young and clean-cut, they thought he was selling drugs."[9]

Seeing her son's frustration, Ma Dukes suggested he channel his anger into his music, resulting in the "Fuck the Police" twelve-inch. Echoing N.W.A.'s controversial song of the same name, the track took Dilla's anger and set it to a relentless drum break and a funky flute loop. Lyrically, the song marked a sharp departure from the laid-back freestyles of Slum Village, openly voicing his disdain for local law enforcement and inviting "any offended people, suck my balls."

"It's getting so crazy in Detroit now with the police, man. I just felt like I wanted to speak on it. People knew it from N.W.A., but I just wanted to touch it on a more underground level so the people that I fuck with can relate too and people know that it's still going on," said Dilla. "It's like you can go through life and act like it's not but I deal with it everyday, for real, just riding in a nice car they'll fuck with you. Just being a black person in Detroit, it's so stupid."[10]

Due in part to its honesty, and in part to *that beat*, the song was embraced by the hip-hop underground and remains a cherished moment in Dilla's solo career: "[P]eople are still singing it today!" said Ma Dukes, "Every time I go somewhere, that's one of the songs they play."[11]

Not everything he did was met with the usual acclaim from listeners, however. Dilla had already dealt with fans that were ill prepared for the different direction found on the final two Tribe albums. After three certified classics, fans expected more of the youthful exuberance they were used to. Instead, they got the somber and somewhat weary insights of a group that was maturing as artists and growing apart as individuals. Further complicating matters was the change in sound, bringing Dilla's woozy drum patterns and re-assembled chops to a group always heralded for its precision looping of four-bar samples. It's not that *Beats, Rhymes and Life* or *The Love Movement* are bad albums, they were just different; Questlove later likened it to, "advanced calculus being taught to a class that just recently mastered algebra."[12]

"[He was] changing the course of people's careers, which was at the time quote-unquote for the worse," said Ronnie Reese, a journalist who has written about Dilla's career extensively. "Like with Tribe, people heard *Beats, Rhymes and Life*, and *The Love Movement* and were like, 'Man, this doesn't sound like old Tribe.' And looking back, you realize how brilliant it was."

As the new man in the crew, Dilla ended up taking most of the heat from fans who didn't want their favorite group to change, a criticism that persisted for years afterwards: In 2009, one hip-hop blog looked back on *Beats* with the blunt sub-head, "Did Dilla Destroy A Tribe Called Quest?" (the writer concluded he did not; many commenters disagreed). When Q-Tip veered in a decidedly more commercial direction for his solo debut *Amplified*, fan distaste only increased. It would not be the last time Dilla would be accused of "destroying" a beloved artist.

By the time Common started work on the follow-up to *Like Water for Chocolate*, he was ready to cut loose and push his art wherever he could. Inspired by both his fellow Soulquarians and recording in New York's historic Electric Lady studios, 2002's *Electric Circus* threw rock, funk, soul, and even ragtime jazz into a blender, making for a raucous and eclectic album that was more ambitious than most were prepared for.

"A lot of people didn't really understand the *Electric Circus* album, but coming up with some of the music for that was crazy. Common wanted to go to the next level and be really experimental, and we were going there," said keyboardist James Poyser, a member of the Soulquarians who played on the project. "That was an amazing time. There was so much music we made that couldn't possibly be used for anything else, because it was so left field—things with different tempos, different time signatures. It was just really creative—extra creative. We tried to go as far as possible with it."[13]

"When we started to do Common's [album], he was like, 'Nah, man. I'm putting the drums away. I'm putting all that African sound away, and I'm going straight Kraftwerk; you coming with me?'" said Questlove. "At that point, it had taken me six years to establish a trademark sound, which everyone now instantly knew ... But he was like, 'Nah, man. Let's go the opposite. Go the complete opposite of what you would do.' And I was just like, 'Why?' He was like, 'Cause, man, this is what you gotta do. Everyone has now caught up to what you're doing, and for you to stay ahead of the pack, you're going to have to get uncomfortable and just go there.'"[14] While *Electric Circus* scored a healthy level of critical approval, the public seemed baffled, and the record was a commercial failure.

Never one to sweat public opinion much, Dilla seemed uncharacteristically stung by the album's reception in a 2005 interview: "[W]hat people don't understand is ... when I go in the studio, I just try to give the artist what they want. With *Like Water for Chocolate*, we were both looking toward the direction of where he started or what would have been rugged hip-hop at that time. Then with *Electric Circus*, he wanted to do something totally different. I would bring him a batch of beats, and he'd just be sitting there, then as soon as I make something crazy as hell, up-tempo, he'd be like, 'Yeah, let's use that one.' I don't want people to think this is all I'm giving him. I gotta give him what he wants. It's kind of hard to read those reviews knowing that they don't understand that shit."[15]

Life on a major label wasn't working out as well as he would have liked, either. He'd signed a one-year deal on MCA with an option for a second, provided he turned in two albums the label accepted for release. Instead of repeating the format he'd used on *Welcome 2 Detroit*, he didn't plan to produce any of the music for his sophomore solo effort; he just wanted to rap over beats by other producers. Any beats he made for MCA were set aside for the second project, a full-length album titled *48 Hours* by his childhood friends Frank Bush and Derrick Harvey, who performed together as the duo Frank-n-Dank.

Why would an artist signed on the strength of his production work choose not to produce any of the music on his next solo effort? Why would an artist with his connections opt to produce an album for a pair of rappers few outside of Detroit had ever heard of?

The latter question might be easier to answer. By 2002 Dilla was at a point in his career where he could devote his energies to projects he was passionate about, and his passions were sending him back to the underground (and turning down offers from the likes of N*SYNC, Diddy, and Dr. Dre). The early endorsement from Tribe, association with The Soulquarians and his decision to make music oppositional to what was popular at the time meant he'd been saddled with the "backpacker" label, even though his sensibilities were always more corner than conscious. As Dilla recalled to *XXL* in 2004:

> It was kinda fucked up [getting that stamp] because people automatically put us in that [Tribe] category. That was actually a category that we didn't actually wanna be in. I thought the music came off like that, but we didn't realize that shit then. I mean, you gotta listen to the lyrics of the shit, niggas was talking about getting head from bitches. It was like a nigga from Native Tongues never woulda said that shit. I don't know how to say it, it's kinda fucked up because the audience we were trying to give to were actually people we hung around. Me, myself, I hung around regular ass Detroit cats. Not the backpack shit that people kept putting out there like that. I mean, I ain't never carried no goddamn backpack, but like I said, I understand to a certain extent. I guess that's how the beats came off on some smooth type of shit … and there was a lot of hard shit on the radio so our thing was we're gonna do exactly what's not on the radio.[16]

Working with Frank-n-Dank not only gave Dilla the chance to give his childhood friends an opportunity to share in his good fortune, it also gave him the chance to reconnect with the part of himself looking to hang with "regular ass Detroit cats."

The decision to dedicate his solo project to rhyming may have been more personal. While Dilla's musical output was typically well received, his skills as a rapper were less warmly embraced (*SPIN* magazine claimed in 2000 he "may be the worst rapping producer since Warren G";[17] the AllMusic Guide called the rappers dated and uninteresting[18]).

"Nobody was really feeling [Slum Village] lyrically, in comparison to the beats that Dilla was making," said Ronnie Reese. "People didn't really understand the style of rapping that Dilla, Baatin, and T3 were doing. Coming out of that classic Rakim, Gang Starr mentality, you hear Slum for the first time you're like *What the fuck is this?*"

Despite the criticisms, MC'ing was an essential part of Dilla's musical identity, a way to let loose, to have fun with the music in a way that his relentless creative drive might not have allowed.

"Definitely an alter ego," said Karriem Riggins. "He called him Niggaman ... he'd start talking about 'Yo, I got the [Range Rover] ... with the fifth wheel on the back, that was Niggaman all day.'"[19] Dilla even calls the alias out explicitly on *Welcome 2 Detroit*'s "Shake it Down."

The MCA album would have been a deliberate thwarting of expectations, and Dilla recruited an impressive roster of producers he knew and admired to provide beats, including Pete Rock, a young Kanye West and a rising underground star from Los Angeles named Madlib.

"That would have been his defining moment," said House Shoes. "Everyone was fronting on his lyrics."[20]

His defining moment would have to wait. The absorption of MCA by Geffen Records the year after Dilla signed his deal left him and other hip-hop acts in the wind; turnover in the A&R department was so frequent no one knew who was responsible for what, and both projects ended up shelved.

Frustrated and fed up, Dilla threw himself into music for its own sake, crafting the songs that would make up the *Ruff Draft* EP (allegedly in a week) with a deliberate aesthetic in mind, a philosophy explicitly outlined in the album's introduction. *Ruff Draft* was for people who wanted "real live shit," but more tellingly, was to "sound like it's straight from the motherfuckin' cassette." In ten tracks over 20 short minutes, Dilla again overturned any expectations fans and listeners might have had about what his sound should be. As was his habit, he looked at the clean, sleek production of The Neptunes, Dr. Dre, and Irv Gotti, turned around and walked in the opposite direction. Live instrumentation was put back on the shelf in a return to sampling obscure, experimental synth, disco, and rock records. He coated the songs in a film of tape hiss. He abandoned traditional song structures, tracks could alternately have no hooks ("Let's Take It Back") or consist of nothing but ("Nothing Like This"). Lyrically, the album was a mission statement designed to finally separate himself from the ideas people had of him based on who he worked with, rapping "and these backpackers wanna confuse it cause niggas is icy, it ain't got nothing to do with the music," on "Make'em NV."

He pressed a small run of vinyl with his own money and released it on his own Mummy Records label, scoring distribution through Groove Attack, a tiny German distributor now one of the largest in Europe. Dilla found the experience of working with small, independent labels to be far preferable to the machinery of a major. His comments around that time seem to presage the direction the music industry would trend toward, at a time when online distribution was seen as more of a threat than a tool.

"You know, if I had a choice, skip the major labels and just put it out yourself man!" he said in a 2002 interview.

"I tell everybody it's better to do it yourself and let the indies come after you instead of going in there and getting a deal and you have to wait. It ain't fun, take it from me. Right now, I'm on MCA but it feels like I'm an unsigned artist still. It's cool, it's a blessing, but damn I'm like, 'When's my shit gonna come out? I'm ready now, what's up?' They're just like they gotta wait on this person and this person and they're firing this person. It's getting crazy. I woulda did a lot better just not even fucking with them, keep doing what I was doing before."[21]

Hard lessons weren't the only takeaway from the MCA experience, however; it also sparked the creative partnerships that would define the remaining years of Dilla's life.

There's a video of Dilla, Frank, Dank, and Common in Dilla's home studio in Michigan's Clinton Township, date unknown, likely 2003. Frank and Dank are acting as hosts, narrating what's going on, taking the camera on a tour of the facility, showing off the pool table, the vocal booth, the drum room filled with records. In the video's closing moments the duo are swapping stories to Common about how they would go dancing when they were younger. And in the back corner, seated by a turntable and his MPC sampler, is Dilla, laughing as his friends clown and crack jokes. He's obviously paying attention to the conversation, but his hands *never stop moving*. He puts records on the turntable, places the needle, listens for what only he knows he wants, removes the record, meticulously places it back in its sleeve and into a protective plastic bag. He looks, to a certain extent, like a man apart.[22]

It's isolating, being a genius. To devote that much energy to your craft, to obsess over it, to commit to the Gladwellian 10,000 hours and master it in the way that Dilla had means there are large parts of yourself that other people, even your closest friends, are never going to understand, part of you will always remain unknown. It's a rift of necessity; for artists to create at that caliber they have to sequester themselves from everything but their art. For an artist to meet someone who can create at his level, someone he can respect as a peer, not elevate as an idol, is to find someone who understands that which defines him at his core. Meeting someone like that could change your life.

In many ways, Dilla and Otis "Madlib" Jackson were the mirror images of each other from opposite sides of the country. Prolific beatmakers well versed across genres; celebrated for their music but maligned for their MC'ing; reserved, silent types who only spoke when they had something to say. They were that rarest of things, artists each confident enough in their own abilities to see the other as an inspiration, not a threat. They were Byron and Shelley, Basquiat and Haring, or (to borrow and tweak an analogy Madlib once used) Coltrane and Miles.

After hearing Madlib's work on his group Lootpack's debut album, Dilla invited him to fly out to Detroit in 2001 and work on his vocal project.

"Just to know that Madlib did that stuff on the SP1200 [drum machine/sampler] freaked me out because the only cat I knew that could really freak that machine was Pete Rock," Dilla told *URB* magazine in 2004. "That [Lootpack] album was crazy. Me and my partners rode that shit for the longest time. As soon as I popped my deal with MCA, I went looking for him."

Speaking on *Fan-tas-tic Vol. 1*, Madlib told the same interviewer, "At that time, I ain't heard no producers like that, doing the same shit as me. It was completely different from my stuff but still the same, you know? Like it's always raw and soulful and it never sounds too computerized."[23]

In Dilla's beats, Madlib found something that inspired him in a way nothing else had: "I can't rap to too many other people's beats, and I can barely rap to my own. But when I hear his shit, there's just something to it that I connect with. I could just write to it all day."[24]

At the time of their first meeting, Madlib was working primarily with the indie label Stones Throw Records. After starting as a means for founder Chris "Peanut Butter Wolf" Manak to release music he made with his late friend Charles "Charizma" Hicks, by 2000 Stones Throw had moved from the Bay Area to L.A. and centered around the four-man team of Wolf, graphic designer Jeff Jank, General Manager Eothen "Egon" Alapatt, and Madlib as the marquee artist. Their base of operations was a house in the Mount Washington neighborhood where the four lived, complete with a 1950s-era bomb shelter Madlib used as a studio.

Dilla's reputation on the West Coast was already established by that point, with L.A.'s underground community embracing him with an enthusiasm his hometown never did.

"Back then, like '96, early '97, there was already a community of Dilla heads," said J. Rocc, co-founder of L.A.'s Beat Junkies DJ crew. "So [demos were] already floating around. I told Madlib I had one … so I dubbed it for him, [and] he went and made a bunch of songs over those beats."[25]

One of those songs was eventually called "The Message," and featured Madlib freestyling over one of the most notorious beats in Dilla's career, a flip of Stereolab's "Come and Play in the Milky Night," previously used officially by Busta Rhymes on 2000's "Show Me What You Got."

"I remember at the time [photographer] B+ was the one hipping us to it, like, 'Man, you guys aren't listening to Stereolab?'" Egon recalled. "I'm like, 'Man, that's the shit that the fucking kids at my college radio station are listening to. I'm playing boom-bap hip-hop, or funk,' … [But Dilla] was grabbing from everything and Madlib was the same … you know, no boundaries, that was just the way those guys worked."[26]

In 2002 Peanut Butter Wolf was working on a mixtape compilation and decided to include "The Message" as an exclusive. Wanting to be able to play it when he DJ'd, and digital software not yet being the standard, Wolf pressed up a couple hundred copies as a white-label vinyl release.

"We didn't even tell Dilla, actually, when we did it, and Dilla called me up afterwards like, 'Yo, what's up with the bootleg, man?!' And I wasn't sure if he was like, 'What's up?' like, 'I'm pissed off at you,'" recalled Wolf, "And he was like, 'Yo, man, let's do some shit like that but official.' So we came up with the idea of Madlib rapping over Dilla beats for half the album and Dilla rapping over Madlib beats for the other."[27]

Jeff Jank remembered the discussion being a little more tense. "So when Dilla heard about it he calls up Wolf and chews him out. 'That ain't how you do it, if you want to do something, do it the right way.' The plan to do a Jaylib record was sparked right then and there ... If Dilla didn't have the balls to call Wolf and chew him out, there would have been no collab. I always had a lot of respect for Dilla from that, I mean, he was totally right. We all learned from it."

Even though Madlib and Dilla worked on what would become 2003's *Champion Sound* separately, sending CDs from their respective cities, the mutual impact they were having on each other gave the album a surprisingly unified feel.

Said Egon, "Dilla and Madlib had this energy that they shared and it was obvious when they were doing the Jaylib project that the music they were sending back and forth was influencing the music that they were making. A lot of that was vocal performances but subtly you could hear it in the beats that Dilla would send through and the beats Madlib would send to Dilla."[28]

For the crew at Stones Throw, unfamiliar with the stylistic shift Dilla started working through on *Ruff Draft*, the selections he made from the beats offered to him were surprising but thrilling.

"[T]he way that he would pick Madlib's tracks, you would think he would go through three hundred Madlib beats and would be picking some of the more slick ... commercial sounding beats," said Egon. "He went for the grimiest of the grimy Madlib beats and flipped em. And now all of a sudden you find a lot of people trying to record music like that but at the time he was saying this is relevant on a commercial scale."[29]

While *Champion Sound* was well received in the press it ended up being overshadowed by another of

Madlib's projects: Madvillain, his collaboration with the enigmatic, metal-masked rapper MF Doom. Their album *Madvillainy* quickly became one of Stones Throw's highest-selling albums and most critically acclaimed.

"This whole [Jaylib] thing was happening while Madvillain was being created. But for Madvillain there was a huge buzz, we were about to have our first hit," said Jeff Jank. "Jaylib was cool, but no hit … I mean, it got around, people know it and love it, but more on an underground level."

Sales notwithstanding, the project allowed Dilla to fully commit to a style that would inform where he later went on *Donuts*: a return to straight loops and samples with both feet planted firmly in the underground.

"You know, I think with the Jaylib record he was able to do something totally off the fucking cuff, like you know, it gets released as an album in short order with no one telling him, 'You need to change this, oh you need to change that.' I think he felt like, 'Oh wow there's something here,'" said Egon. "I think he got a cool vibe from [us]. I think he thought we were a little bit tighter of a family than we were, you know we were a very dysfunctional family that even then was on the verge of splitting up."

"No one was fucking with Jay at that time," J. Rocc recalled. "There was Busta Rhymes and Common, and De La, but from the end of 2002 through 2003, if you look at his discography, there's nothing but independent shit. He went back to his roots, basically. He went 360."[30]

***

Dilla's collaborations with Madlib may have brought a renewed sense of focus to his musical output after his experience at MCA, but there were distractions of a personal nature he couldn't ignore.

After a European tour to promote the release of *Ruff Draft*, Dilla stepped off the plane feeling like he had the flu. He drove to his parents' house, complaining of nausea and chills. When he didn't improve, Ma Dukes took him to the emergency room in neighboring Grosse Pointe, Michigan. According to the *Detroit Free Press*, Dilla's blood platelet[31] count was below 10, when it should have been between 140 and 180. He shouldn't have been able to even stand. A specialist later delivered the diagnosis of TTP. Dilla stayed at the hospital for a month and a half, only to return a few weeks later with the same complaints. He would occasionally rally enough to travel to L.A. and shoot a Jaylib video (looking heavy from the medications he was on) or to do a short tour through North America with other Stones Throw artists, but he would always get sick again. Despite the frequent hospital stays, when Common offered him the chance to move out to Los Angeles with him, he took the invitation.

"I thought Southern California would be good for his spirits," said Common, "the sun, the warmth, the beautiful women."[32]

To some on the West Coast, it seemed a sudden and surprising decision for someone who held down his city as fiercely as he did.

"Dilla was synonymous with Detroit for all of us," said Egon. "[A]ll of us kind of regarded him as a mythic figure … He would pop into these different cities but he was clearly Detroit."[33]

But the love Dilla had for his city sometimes felt like a one-sided relationship, telling journalists he considered the city's hip-hop scene to be at "zero percent," as far back as 1999.[34] He started to notice differences in reception when he took a rare moment away from his studio to travel, telling a reporter in Toronto, "It's weird, in Detroit I'm just a regular joe. But you go to New York or Cali or London, even coming to Toronto now; it's a whole different thing. I get the love for what I do in that basement, it's like appreciated so I go back and do more shit. But it's hard in the D 'cause you gotta come with a commercial-ass single to get played or get noticed, or you gotta be hard as hell and talk about killing somebody."[35]

"You know, when you get older, you look for a certain type of vibe to do what you do … and maybe Detroit just didn't have it for him anymore. He'd used it up," said Frank.[36]

House Shoes, a Detroit-to-L.A. transplant himself, has never been one to mince words regarding how he feels his hometown treats its artists.

"I've said this shit to people around the world and nobody can wrap their head around it, and that is the fact that nobody in Detroit gives a fuck about Detroit hip-hop. Nobody. Nobody in Detroit knows who Dilla is … it's pretty much a dumb-ass city … having to fucking fight for the respect of your city, it beats you up … Nobody knew who the fuck Dilla was in the city. Dilla could be at the mall, don't nobody know who the fuck he is. He's out [in L.A.], he's signing autographs at the fucking gas station."[37]

Leaving behind the snow and sleet of harsh Michigan winters was its own reward, but a move to California may have allowed Dilla's surroundings to catch up to his creative convictions.

"Detroit's home, but it's good to go out there and feel a different environment and just get an understanding that there's a different way of life than the Midwest," said Ronnie Reese. "Waajeed told me, and I knew this, Detroit's a black city. It's rich in African-American history and African-American culture. I think that's contributed to the greatness of the music that's come out of that area. But you go to L.A. and you see the diversity out there and it just gives you whole new perspectives on creativity because you're being fed things from a number of different cultures ... Coming from where Dilla was ... making the type of beats that he was making with Boz Skaggs records and Tomita and shit like that, mentally in a sense, he was already there."

The move would also allow Dilla the chance to continue exploring a creative relationship that had already proven to be extremely rewarding.

"I honestly think Madlb was a big reason why he moved here," said Wolf. "I never talked to him about it, and there's no way to confirm or deny that, but that's just how I felt about it."[38]

Ronnie Reese added, "Dilla really had no peers other than Madlib. Even outside of music, you have two cats who love to smoke weed, love to go to strip clubs. They bonded in a number of different ways."

"When he moved to L.A., we hung out all the time. We talked all the time. That's the only dude I talked to; I don't pick my phone up," said Madlib.[39]

That camaraderie extended to the rest of the Stones Throw team, as well as others like J. Rocc, who DJ'd and toured with Jaylib, his Beat Junkies crewmate Rhettmatic, and Dave NewYork, a luxury car rental agent who built a strong reputation in the hip-hop community.

"Everybody loved him," said J. Rocc, "We were like his second family, more or less, in addition to the family he's got in the D, like House Shoes and those cats. Out here, it was like, bam! You're down. You're Dilla—if you're down, we're rolling with you."[40]

Ma Dukes also noticed how readily the Golden State embraced her son: "Detroit will look at you and let you go—they don't embrace you. In Los Angeles, it's totally different. The love there is like you were born and raised there ... Maybe it's because we have so many people here that are talented, that we take them for granted, and it takes something like people leaving here for us to look."[41]

Thrilled as they were to have him out in L.A., nobody at the time knew the reason for the move, or how bad his condition could get.

Jeff Jank recalled, "There was a time in late 2004, Egon and I were over at Madlib's studio in Echo Park, not too long after he moved from the house where the four of us lived. Madlib says Dilla had driven over to see him, they probably smoked, went through a bunch of records ... So Dilla leaves, and Madlib stayed in the studio a few more hours before leaving himself. But when he goes outside, Dilla is still in the front seat of his car. You see, there was something wrong with him. We had no idea what was going on, and hadn't thought much of it at the time because we'd seen him looking good and enjoying life in L.A. But soon after that he started one of his lengthy stays at [Cedars Sinai]." Not long after, Dilla called his mother requesting she go to Los Angeles to help him out. She stayed with him until he passed.

Dilla started 2005 at Cedars, prompting some websites to erroneously report he'd been rushed to the emergency room and was in a coma. With most of his people back in Detroit, Ma Dukes reached out to the crew in L.A.

According to Egon, "One day ... she said, 'Look, there's going to be times where he's good and there's going to be times when's he's bad,'— and this was before anyone knew how serious things were—she was like, 'If he's in a good way, you can just come by.'

"And I think to myself, well that's kind of weird, you know? I run this record company, we put out his records, I'm not trying to be that dude. She's like, 'You need to come by. Somebody needs to come by, his friends need to come by.' And so I just said, you know what, I'm just going to take this at face value, I'm not going to be a fucking weirdo about it I'm just going to go in there and do whatever it is that you do, sitting in a hospital room. So I started going."

The Stones Throw circle soon began visiting Dilla on a regular basis during his hospital stays. They celebrated his birthday there in February 2005, sneaking a cake into his room. They brought him video games, copies of whatever they were working on, portable samplers, and turntables. They watched *Napoleon Dynamite* with him. Most importantly, they brought music, the one thing he couldn't do without. This crew of exceptional oddballs rallied around Dilla, not out of obligation to some professional working relationship, but because they respected the man as the greatest producer of his generation and felt he didn't deserve to be alone.

"He was in the hospital for about eight months to a year. Not moving. Couldn't leave the room, ain't no get up and go for a walk, ain't none of that shit," said J. Rocc, "It was like, you show up, Ma Dukes was already there chilling—'Aw, you're here, I'm going to go take a break, all right, I'll see you later.' And it was just him in the bed. With a sampler right here, and a stack of 45s. And whatever we would bring him. We would show up, aw man Madlib, let's go bring him some records, or Egon, or yo, Wolf, what you got for him? … [E]veryone was coming out for him."[42]

"I think you know, in some weird way … he probably thought we were all sort of misfits in one way or another, but then again he didn't necessarily fit in where he was. And he loved Los Angeles, he loved hanging out in the sunshine, and he loved kicking it with Madlib," said Egon. "You know it was just like, one of those things, man. We were just fucking there at the right time, and it was very unfortunate because it was the wrong time, too."

Workinonit

From the outside looking in, it might have seemed as though Dilla's musical output had slowed down much more considerably than it had. Aside from a pair of tracks he contributed to *Be*, Common's quote–unquote comeback album in 2005, what little material released publicly was with independent or underground acts like Talib Kweli or other Stones Throw artists like MED and Madlib's brother Oh No. But he continued working on beats whenever his health would permit. He'd worked out a deal to do another album for BBE, and spent most of his time working on the project, a true follow-up to *Welcome 2 Detroit* where he would produce all of the music and share rhyming duties with collaborators. And he still "practiced," filling CDs with beats, working his way through yet another shift in style.

While the music he was making during the L.A. years continued to feature the dusty drums and lower fidelity first found on *Ruff Draft*, he replaced the synths and electronic sounds with acoustic instruments and soulful vocal samples. Soul samples had seen a revival since Kanye West and Just Blaze used them throughout Jay-Z's album *The Blueprint* in 2001, but Dilla came at them from an entirely different angle.

An early indication of where he was at musically can be found on "Dollar," by British electronic artist Steve Spacek. Built around a 12-second sample of "Let the Dollar Circulate" by Philadelphia soul singer Billy Paul, Dilla snags a moment of Paul's vibrato delivery of the word "circulate," and stretches it through the length of an entire verse, turning his voice into an hypnotic, indecipherable drone. Unlike the way in which they were used by his contemporaries, Dilla's use of soul vocals accented the melodies of the composition, he never looped them: Instead, he stripped them down into their most basic elements, slicing, stretching, and bending them into bizarre and compelling new forms.

"It was a more mature version of that Kanye West school of production, with the chipmunk voices and using vocals as part of the melody," said Rich Medina, a DJ and member of New York's legendary Rocksteady Crew. "Like, 'Nah B, hold on. Y'all niggas some Toyotas. Here's the Mercedes.' Even if he didn't mean it that way, that's what it sounded like to me."[1]

The shift in sound during his time in L.A. may have had practical reasons as well: "He only came to L.A. with the [MPC] and that was basically it. And then whatever Otis would buy him and whatever else he would buy at Guitar Center," said J. Rocc.[2] Having left a sophisticated studio setup back in Detroit, if Dilla was going to keep making music, he'd have to do it on what he could take with him. And since the days of Camp Amp and Davis Aerospace, hardware limitations were just problems to be solved, so it wasn't long before new beat batches started circulating through the city.

"He was always giving us beat tapes and he was making kind of jokey names for them, one of them was called *Pizza Man*, one was *Donuts*, and it was always this unhealthy food," said Wolf. "I just remember it was me, Madlib and him in the car, and he was like, 'here's my new stuff.' … He played it and I wasn't sure if it was supposed to be a beat tape for rappers or what it was supposed to be, but to me it sounded like the songs were full, finished songs, and I said we should put this out as it is."[3]

Everyone at Stones Throw agreed the music that would end up on *Donuts* was exceptional (Jank remembered thinking it was the best beat tape he'd ever heard), but Egon had some reservations; he was more interested in pursuing a follow-up to *Champion Sound*.

"If it wasn't for Chris, *Donuts* wouldn't [have] happened because Chris said, 'We're making an instrumental record around Jay Dee because that's all he can do.' I was the first person to say 'That's ridiculous, you need to get the next Jaylib record done because the Jaylib record is the one that made him healthy during his first bout with lupus.' And Chris is like, 'No, we're going to do an instrumental record because it's all he can do, that's what we're going to do.' Period, full stop."

There was one problem: Because it had originated as a "beat tape," short sketches of the kind producers would use to shop their work to rappers and labels, the CD Dilla had given them was only 22 minutes long.

"[S]o the *Donuts* beat CD comes around and I really remember it as being a mutual understanding that we wanted to release this as a record … It's a little out of the ordinary for a label to put out a whole record of beats, some of which could potentially be profitable for the producer later on, but we decide to wing it," said Jank.

"The only question is, how is this 22-minute CD with some rugged transitions going to become a record? Dilla wasn't saying he was going to turn it into an album overnight, and Wolf and Egon weren't going to work on it, I think because they were both a little afraid of making a wrong turn and getting on Dilla's bad side."

Dilla's temper was no secret to those who knew him. While not quick to anger, he didn't hesitate to voice his opinion if he thought he'd been slighted: he let Wolf have it over the Jaylib bootleg; he chewed Egon out for inadvertently letting it slip to someone outside the circle that he was hospitalized; he almost came to blows with House Shoes over a crate of records, prompting him to slide a diss into his verse on the Jaylib song "Strapped."

"If you was really fucking with Jay, it wasn't always a bed of roses," said Shoes.[4] "We'd be in the studio and there'd be like some hoe-ass business shit going on that he'd be upset about, and then somebody completely unrelated to that would call and he would just go in on a motherfucker."

Even Ma Dukes could acknowledge her son was not without his moments: "He got stronger, I guess from the knocks of coming along in [the music industry], and he became just outright belligerent at times. He never backed down ... we would get neck and neck sometimes."[5]

With Egon and Wolf not looking to press their luck, there was one person left on the label side to act as liaison and guide the project.

"I never had my chance to get on his bad side, so I became the exec[utive] producer," said Jank. "The process from [there] was, which other music to include to make it longer—without changing what we loved about the original—and a process of editing, mastering, and whatnot. This happened entirely when Dilla was at Cedars."[6]

There were business concerns as well. Stones Throw was a small label, but they wanted to figure out a means to ensure Dilla was properly compensated. So, in the sort of move that could only fly somewhere like Stones Throw, they worked out a deal where the label would retain the product of *Donuts* the album as an asset, but Dilla was still free to take the beats contained therein and shop them to other artists.

"It was a very open-ended deal, you know," said Egon, "it was meant to say ... you're a working musician, we will market a beat tape for you. You can sell the beats, you can do whatever you want, and we're just going to put this out, because we believe in you."

If anything, *Donuts* emerged as a sort of unanticipated side project. The primary focus was *The Shining*, his follow-up to *Welcome 2 Detroit* on BBE, most of which was completed in 2004. Trying to chart an accurate chronology for the music of that time is difficult at best; when a man is known for building beats in 15 minutes, and is consistently ahead of the curve, keeping it all straight becomes nigh impossible. Jank remembered going to meet Dilla once and having him hand over a disc with seven new beats on it that would end up comprising the last half of *Donuts*. Whether they were newly created, or older works he thought fit the mood of the album, is unclear.

"He was always concerned with getting out the beats he'd made in 2002 and 2003 which still seemed new. Like that MED beat [2005's 'Push'], he probably made that beat in 2001," said Egon.[7]

Even though they weren't working on anything official, the spiritual connection between Dilla and Madlib continued as well. During one hospital visit, Jank brought Dilla a copy of *The Further Adventures of Lord Quas*, by Madlib's helium-voiced alter ego Quasimoto.

"He asked me on the spot if I'd do the cover for *The Shining*, 'with some of this Quasimoto type shit.' So I originally planned to have those two albums linked in some way. I put Dilla on the cover of *Further Adventures* and drew a foldout that would match a foldout for *The Shining*. But that ended up going into *Donuts*."[8] Indeed, when placed together, the interior art of both albums line up to form two blocks of a slightly surreal Los Angeles, from the crowds flowing out of "Dilla's Donuts," down the street from the chain-smoking aardvark, Quasimoto himself, checking out the Blaxploitation flicks being shown at the Pussycat Theatre.

Jank recalled, "It's incredible to think about now, but he had this crazy full-face mask at the hospital for some procedure, and he wanted a photo of that on his album cover [for *The Shining*]. I took a picture of it!"[9]

It was a difficult time. Dilla's kidney function had dropped significantly; dialysis became a regular part of his life, three times a week. Long periods spent sedentary in a hospital bed weakened his legs; he would get around with a walker or cane, sometimes a wheelchair. The diagnosis of lupus came just before his thirty-first birthday in 2005. But he refused to be limited by his condition. Dr. Aron Bick, Dilla's hematologist in L.A., told the *Detroit Free Press*, "He didn't want to be a professional patient. The treatment was difficult because he would not want to go to the hospital. He was very intelligent. He said, 'I hear you, doc. But here are my decisions about my own life.'

"I admired that on a human level. He got the medical care he needed. He really did not let his medical situation handicap his life. To him, life came first. He made peace with himself before we even knew it."[10]

When Madlib and photographer/filmmaker Brian "B+" Cross offered him an invitation to tag along on their trip to a film festival in Brazil, Dilla enthusiastically accepted, even if it quickly became apparent his body wasn't up for it.

"[H]e was just hype, 'Hell yeah, I wanna do it.' But we didn't realize how sick he was," said Cross. "So we picked him up from the house and I noticed when we took him out to the car he looked kind of bent over a bit and he looked very weak … [We realized] he was far too weak to be traveling. He shouldn't have been traveling. Put his life in danger basically."[11]

Dilla made it through three days on the trip, seeing the sights and digging for records before he had to be flown back to L.A. on an ambulance flight to Cedars-Sinai. "His hand swelled up like—Madlib called it the 'Hulk hand'—His hand just swelled the fuck up. Like he was really in pain and … he locked himself in the hotel room," said Egon.

His sudden and unexpected return to L.A. derailed another reason for the trip: Stones Thrown had asked B+ to snap some photos for the cover of *Donuts*. Back in the hospital, and in his current condition, taking new photos wasn't an option, and the label already went through what photos they had promoting Jaylib. So Jank reached out to Andrew Gura, a Los Angeles-based video director who had done the clip for MED's Dilla-produced song "Push." In the long tradition of hip-hop videos but a rare move for him, Dilla made a cameo appearance, so Jank asked Gura if there were any stills from the shoot that could be used. He sent back three, including one of Dilla with his head in a downward tilt, laughing at a joke he and MED cracked moments before, his face half-covered by a Detroit Tigers fitted cap. It was a compromise to circumstance, now considered by many to be an iconic image.[12]

Stones Throw's mandate for the album is clear in the rest of the cover's design: remind the public of who he was. It uses both the "J Dilla" *and* "Jay Dee" monikers, and (on early pressings) included a one-sentence rundown of his notable collaborations, as well as quotes extolling his greatness from the biggest hit makers of the time, Pharrell Williams and Kanye West.

By October 2005, *Donuts* was ready for release, but Stones Throw hit a roadblock in their supply chain. Their distributor, EMI, didn't think a weird, difficult instrumental album by an underground producer would move the projected 10,000 copies.

"That wasn't just some loser at EMI, that was like people that we respected, that believed in Stones Throw … and they were like, 'It ain't gonna happen,'" said Egon. "You know to be fair to them, *Champion Sound* had flopped … it had just absolutely and utterly flopped. For a company like Stones Throw, that was next to disastrous." Coming to an agreement with the distributor pushed the album's release back to early 2006.

With the album finished, Dilla was already looking to his next move, one few could have predicted. In early December 2005 he boarded a plane and flew overseas for a short series of European dates with Frank-n-Dank and Phat Kat. His health had deteriorated so much he had to travel confined to a wheelchair, but he refused to allow a silly thing like standing prevent him from rocking a crowd, performing songs from *Welcome 2 Detroit* and *Champion Sound* while in the chair. As reports and photos began to circulate, the public received a rare glimpse at the effects his illness had wrought.

"For somebody who was so concerned with keeping his health kind of to himself, or keeping it a secret, I was really surprised that he did that. It showed so much character," said Wolf.[13]

For Dilla, the trip to Europe was a chance, in some ways, to close a circle, to see the world with friends old and new (Ma Dukes, Rhettmatic of the Beat Junkies, and Dave NewYork accompanied him on the trip) and perform for crowds that had always supported him.

"It was like his farewell tour. It was postponed like twice, and he was the one who wanted to do it," said Phat Kat. "We did that because that's what Dilla wanted to do … and in between, you know, days we had off, he'd go on dialysis. I mean, this nigga was a fucking soldier. Still up there every motherfuckin night, spittin. There wasn't no night where he was like, 'Yo, I can't do this,' and even if he had done that, motherfuckas would have understood that. But this dude rocked every night. He was making beats in the hotel room while we were over there."[14]

Frank-n-Dank filmed footage during that tour, released on the *Frank-n-Dank European Vacation* DVD in 2007. Dilla is a supporting player in the film, passing through the background of shots, appearing fully onstage at the shows or in one lengthy segment filmed at an airport. His face is thin and gaunt, angular. His clothing seems extra baggy, almost to the point of absurdity, possibly to disguise how slight his frame had become. When he swings his arms during another telling of the Pharcyde fistfight story, he does so slowly, feebly. But there's a light in his eyes, it's obvious his spirit is energized by the experience, there's an optimism there, of the sort that makes it easy to understand why anyone who knew him then didn't acknowledge the possibility of him not recovering. He also nails every one of his verses.

Having come to an understanding with their distributor, *Donuts* was set for release in early February, 2006. Stones Throw also pressed up a bonus for some retailers, a seven-inch single of "Signs," a beat made at the same time as the *Donuts* batches but never intended for inclusion on the album. There was excitement to finally see the project through to completion, but it was tinged with melancholy.

"When I went to deliver finished copies of the *Donuts* LP, CD, and the [seven-inch], it was one of these days that was not a good time. He'd undergone dialysis, he looked like he was in serious pain, not a good time for visitors," said Jank, "I said my hello and gave him the records because I knew he was looking forward to them. That was maybe Feb 1st. I had to fly to N.Y. right after that, and that was the last I saw him."[15]

Questlove swung through to visit in January 2006, during Grammy week. Even he wasn't fully aware of just how sharply Dilla's health had declined. "When I stepped into his house in California, I was totally unprepared for what I saw. It was just Dilla and his mother, and it really wasn't Dilla at all. In his place was a frail, eighty-pound man in a wheelchair. He couldn't communicate at all. He was mumbling and gesturing weakly … all I knew at the time was what I saw, which was that he was dying."[16]

Donuts was released on Dilla's thirty-second birthday, February 7, 2006. The Stones Throw crew planned a small party at Common's house to celebrate: Madlib, Wolf, J. Rocc, and Egon, who arrived late after picking up a donut-shaped cake.

"I pull up to the house with the fucking cake, and I see Madlib and he's looking at me shaking his head. And I'm like, 'What are you doing outside?' And [Wolf] looks at me and he was just like, 'You can't go in,' … and I was like, 'What do you mean I can't go in?' He's like, 'Yo, really. This is really, really fucking bad.'"

"At that point I really felt like something was wrong, more so than ever," said Wolf. "Even a few weeks before that he was in a wheelchair, but he was energetic and showing me music and showing me his equipment and talked about moving all of his equipment that's still in Detroit to L.A."[17]

Egon recalled, "I felt like I was having a heart attack. Like it was the worst thing I'd ever felt in my life and I was like, 'I gotta go right now,' … [and Wolf is] like 'Fine, then I'm coming with you.' And I went straight to the hospital and checked myself into the emergency room. I was just having an anxiety attack or something you know, or whatever. But my chest caved in."

James Yancey died three days later on February 10, 2006.

Two Can Win

Forget about dying for a minute. Forget about hospital beds and dialysis machines and wheelchairs. It almost seems unfair to do so, that's how intrinsically linked they've become with the album. But put them aside. Imagine finding the album in a record store during that three-day window between its release and the day he died. How is one meant to listen to *Donuts*? How does it process?

> [T]he album's credited to Dilla, but what does that even really mean, given how he builds his house from other people's bricks while at the same time decoupling the snippets of song, the bits of music, the loops, from their original source … in traditional music, you see (or at least imagine) the source of the sound. If it's Aretha Franklin, you see her holding the microphone at the Fillmore or sitting at the piano pounding out "Spirit in the Dark," and even if you don't see her, you see her …[1]

But what does one "see" as the source of the sounds on *Donuts*? They flicker across the mind as a collage of images, colors, and mood. It's hip-hop as *musique concrète*.

Even knowing all the sample sources doesn't make the sounds any more discernible in one's mind, it only turns the experience of listening to it into an absurdist horror movie: Galt McDermott is peacefully tinkling away on his piano when the Jacksons fall on top of him as though dropped from a flatbed truck in the sky. Michael and his brothers twitch and jerk like androids with faulty wiring, garbling out unintelligible vocal spurts. They bring the tempo down as Lou Rawls pulls himself from the muck of a blackwater swamp to the side of stage left, dragging his wheezing carcass into view before being obliterated by the horns of Gene and Jerry, fired with the intensity of a laser shot from a satellite. The assault is over quickly, but it'll take more than that to finish Lou, who continues his trembling crawl across the stage, commenting on the entire affair: *sure, it's strange* ... No, *Donuts* is a game of resonant emotion, a mind meld between its maker and the listener.

It starts as though in mid-thought, like dropping the needle in the middle of the record; with no previous knowledge the CD might seem faulty. Pianos jingle, his name stutters repeatedly, announcing his arrival. Thirteen seconds to settle in before the accelerating rumble of "Workinonit" explodes like a muscle car roaring across the pavement, heralded by the shriek of a siren.

First heard on *Ruff Draft*, the siren had grown into a sonic signature, a way for him to identify his beats for MCs sorting through piles of unmarked tracks: If you heard it, you knew it was a Dilla beat. It's pulled from a song by New York electro-hop duo Mantronix, a mix of classic breaks and loops not unlike *Donuts* itself: "Amen,

Brother." "Funky Penguin." "Take Me to the Mardi Gras." It's startling and unsettling, conjuring images of air raids, ambulances, and emergencies. The siren appears on nine of the album's 31 beats, one of the few unifying elements to be found.

The first time *Donuts* is heard, it may seem curious what the big deal is. Like his work on "Little Brother," it's easy to mistake it for a series of minimalist loops with a few scratches on top and the occasional flourish of virtuosic chopping. Overrated, all hype. Something like "Lightworks," when compared to the Raymond Scott original, seems like little more than a re-edit with a cleaner mix. But the beat running in the background, nowhere on the original, is a wonder of programming, it's so low in the mix it's easy to miss just how hard it swings; when J. Rocc plays the track in his sets, he often strips away everything else but the drums, letting them ride out for minutes, demonstrating to the audience just how much is going on there.

If you know what he's working with, these moments of stupefying brilliance happen more than once. Did he really lift the drums for "The Twister" from that Stevie Wonder live track? How the hell did he snag clean vocals from James Brown's introduction on "My Thing" to use on "Light My Fire?" How did he turn Luther Ingram's "To the Other Man" into two beats that sound so distinctly different from each other? How does a person's brain listen to the Chicago soul of LV Johnson and decide, "Oh, I'll make 'Airworks' with that"? It makes no sense. If he'd done one of these things, it would have been an inspired achievement but the fact that he does them all, again and again? Stunning.

The album features a cast of recurring characters in addition to the siren. Ad Rock of the Beastie Boys makes cameo appearances on "Workinonit," and "The New." Joeski Love, a rapper who scored a novelty hit in 1986 with "Pee-Wee's Dance" shows up on "Workinonit," "The Twister," and "Anti-American Graffitti." He's the audience stand-in, the Greek Chorus of the album, taking in the pandemonium around him with a confused, "*Huh? What?*" Introductions play a recurring role as well: Numerous tracks feature the sound of someone being welcomed onto the stage, invited to perform, reminding the audience of the performer's accomplishments, just as Dilla was trying to do on this album. But the supporting character with the largest role, however, is error. Mistakes. They happen again and again, tiny glitches that get stuck in the ear: A pinched piano note on "Mash," the start/stop of "Airworks," the microphone feedback on "Dilla Says Go," or the multiple time variations throughout.

J Dilla: "I used to listen to records and actually, I wouldn't say look for mistakes, but when I heard mistakes in records it was exciting for me. Like, 'Damn, the drummer missed the beat in that shit. The guitar went off key for a second.' I try to do that in my music a little bit, try to have that live feel a little bit to it."[2]

Jeff Jank: "[Something] which really seemed much more true with Dilla once I became immersed in this record while it was being edited, is how you don't feel like he's necessarily working with machines. There's a lot of hip-hop and electronic music—even the really good stuff—where you constantly hear the machines. But he uses these source records and the machines as naturally as one would use a bass and drums."

Jay Hodgson, a recording engineer and professor at the University of Western Ontario: "One of the hardest things is that, if you have training, at some point you sound trained. You do what you're supposed to do ... but hip-hop made a virtue of [not knowing], and it's just so fantastically creative ... Here are the tools, no one's really told me what I'm supposed to do with this, but I'm going to use this thing to make music." As an unidentified sample says on "Don't Cry," *I'll show you how my voice has made an unbelievable thing good.*

Hodgson again: "It's common often to do what he's doing, it's uncommon to do it that well, with that much artistry."

As the album progresses, a dichotomy of mood begins to emerge: Each beat can be plotted on a graph with "skullkicking" on one axis and "heartbreaking" on the other; each track containing both colors in varying opacities. It's the transition he works over and over again: "The Twister" into "One-Eleven," "The Factory" into "U-Luv," "Thunder" into "Gobstopper."

The siren takes a break through the middle movements of the album, returning for three consecutive songs starting with "Thunder." But it feels different when it returns, a change that remains through repeated listens. It seems to stop being frightening and begins feeling powerful, not a wail of despair as much as a screaming defiance in the face of an abyss. That siren is an avatar, a primal "I am," from a man sapped of energy in his real life. Who is he? Who he's always been. It's right there in the title of the Mantronix song the siren originated from.

"King of the Beats."

All hail.

Geek Down

Death is the great universal, the thread that connects me, you, Dilla, every living thing on this planet. We are all going to die. This is not something most individuals care to consider. Existence, consciousness itself, is an industry designed to distract us from that fact, the "screen," Tolstoy wrote of in "The Death of Ivan Ilyich." The story's titular character, slowly succumbing to injuries sustained in a fall, tries to distract himself from that truth, but can never outrun it fully: "Suddenly *it* would flash from behind the screen, he would see *it*. *It* flashes, he still hopes *it* will disappear, but he involuntarily senses his side—there sits the same thing, gnawing in the same way, and he can no longer forget it."[1] For many listeners, especially those with at least a passing familiarity with the album's origins, *Donuts* rips down that screen, its music and messages a stark representation of one man confronting the truth of his mortality, which, while true, is a bit of a facile interpretation. Yes, the record is concerned with such matters, but it expresses that concern in a more nuanced and complicated manner, part of a conversation humanity has been having with itself for centuries.

From the moment humans learned how to think critically, they've been thinking critically about death, and most of that thinking centers on whether death is essentially good or bad. The idea is that if one can prove philosophically that death is not *harmful*, it doesn't merit the fear and panic so often associated with it. The ancient Greek philosopher Epicurus worked this lane first, arguing that death is not a thing to be feared because it removes all sensation, all pleasure or pain, from life. Why fear something that cannot "harm" us in any traditional sense? Epicurus's dismissal of death was so absolute it spawned an epitaph used on the graves of many of his followers: "I was not, I was; I am not, I do not care."

The Roman poet Lucretius furthered that idea of death's irrelevance in his "Symmetry Argument," which posited that one's "absence" in death is analogous to the "absence" experienced before birth. You weren't "here" before you were born, and you didn't notice one way or the other, so, not being "here" after you die shouldn't matter either: Waiting to walk onto the stage is no different than stepping off if it. Which makes death, if not necessarily a good thing, not inherently *bad*, either.

It seems sound on the surface, if one can ignore the fact that conscious existence brings with it experience, challenges, victories, heartbreaks, love, pain, and joy. Death, as we currently understand it (read: secularly), obliterates the memory of all past experience and the promise of the future; you'll never get to learn Swedish, visit Morocco, or take breakdance lessons once you're dead. To Epicureans and humanists, this doesn't matter: Death removes all experience, bad and good, and sometimes you just have to take the bitter with the sweet. What we get is all we have, make the most of it and make room for the generation after you. Rational, but not exactly comforting. Or is it?

No modern school of philosophy examined the nature of death and its relationship to life quite like the Existentialists. First explicated by the Danish philosopher Søren Kierkegaard and revitalized by twentieth-century thinkers like Martin Heidegger, Jean-Paul Sartre, and Albert Camus, this philosophy (painting here with an admittedly broad brush) argued that only the individual could bring meaning to life in the face of an absurd world and faceless God: "After two world wars, everyone was ready for a philosophy that could nod to the irrational elements in life; hence, perhaps the immense popularity of both psychoanalysis and existentialism after the abattoir of the twentieth century."[2] What better guide for tackling the question of finding meaning in life when death is certain?

Camus looked at that paradox in his essay "The Myth of Sisyphus." The myth in question concerns a Greek king, condemned by the gods to push an immense boulder to the top of a hill, only for it to roll back down again upon reaching the summit, forcing him to repeat the act for eternity. Camus used the myth as a starting point to address what he considered "the one true philosophical question, and that is suicide. Judging whether life is worth living amounts to answering the fundamental question of philosophy."[3] For Camus, the puzzle to solve was not whether death was good or bad, but whether its reality negated the purpose of living; he wanted to understand why we bother. Sisyphus's sentence is absurdity in action, as, some might argue, is life. But, for Camus, redemption is found in the moment the condemned king makes his descent back to his rock to start again; that moment surges with possibility, and the hope that *maybe this time* … "Where would the torture be, indeed, if at every step the hope of succeeding upheld him?"[4] To Camus, the toil of Sisyphus is no less absurd than that of anyone who sweeps floors, sells stocks, makes music, or writes books, but there is meaning in the struggle, purpose in the toil, a thought echoed by the modern philosopher Todd May: "Imagine trying to live without projects, without a career trajectory, or relationships or hobbies. These are central elements of a human life … we cannot abandon our projects to live in the present. We must integrate them somehow … One can live engaged in the present and yet also be engaged by one's projects that extend into the future."[5] Given what we know of him, continuing to make his music between rounds of dialysis, it's a sentiment Dilla would appear to have shared.

These may be fun puzzles to muse over, but thinking about death in these ways seems to strip away its dignity; how "good" or "bad" death is, embracing life's absurdity and the subtleties of conscious existence likely offers little comfort to a person facing his or her *definite* end. They also approach death as an abstract concept instead of a physical process: Ask even the most stoic man if he's prepared to die and he may say yes; tell him he'll die in an hour and his response may be different. What does death really mean to the dying? What does it mean to sit there, as Dilla did, performing from a wheelchair on the other side of the world and face the thing we're all trying to avoid, to have Ivan Ilyich's screen torn down in front of you? What then? How do you process it, in life and in art?

***

In 1969 Swiss psychiatrist Elisabeth Kübler-Ross formulated one of, if not the most popular perspectives on facing the end of life in her book *On Death and Dying*. Intended as a guide for medical professionals, the book sought to examine how human beings process the knowledge of impending death, so attending physicians and other medical staff could better relate to their patients.

When she was a girl growing up in Switzerland, Kübler-Ross's neighbor fell from a tree, and was not expected to survive his injuries. The neighbor wished to stay in his home, to forgo any treatments or trips to the hospital. No one denied his request. The man talked with his wife and children, left instructions, put his affairs in order. Kübler-Ross and her parents stayed with the man's family until he died, mourning with them. When he passed, there wasn't a viewing, no cosmetic deception to make him look as if he were sleeping; they simply removed the corpse and buried him.

Decades later Kübler-Ross, now a psychiatrist at the University of Chicago Medical Center, witnessed vastly different attitudes toward terminal patients: Clinical, reticent, treating the individual as a series of problems to be solved in the name of extending life. She wasn't entirely sure the methodology was superior: "[A patient] may want one single person to stop for one single minute so he can ask one single question—but he will get a dozen people around the clock, all busily preoccupied with his heart rate, pulse ... his secretions or excretions but not with him as a human being."[6] Kübler-Ross found her colleagues' devotion to clinical distance unsettling, and couldn't shake the idea that it neglected a patient's basic humanity. In 1965 a group of theology students approached her for assistance on a research project they were working on. They wanted to examine death as the biggest crisis in human life, but were unsure how to collect any data. Her suggestion was simple: If you want to know about death, talk to the dying.

Kübler-Ross and the students began interviewing terminal patients, asking them how they felt about their experiences with doctors, family members, and their own mortality. The more they talked, the more she began to notice patterns emerging, a similarity of experience among them. Her findings entered the popular consciousness as the five-stage "Kübler-Ross Model," which is still used as an aid in understanding the process of confronting death. It's also useful in understanding and interpreting the chaotic mood switches of *Donuts*.

Like most details about *Donuts*, accounts vary on how accurate the "deathbed creation" legend actually is. A 2006 article in *The Source* reported Dilla completed 29 of the album's 31 tracks in the hospital, though "completed" has often been erroneously interpreted as "created."

"[T]here was always like a little box of 45s, stuff like that, but most of the record, almost all of it was made before he got to the hospital," said Egon. "But it was *edited* in the hospital ... [he'd have] his computer out and his headphones on and he'd be editing … He would be in there making the final mix of the record." Adjusting the levels, mixing the sounds and adding effects could have taken as long or longer than chopping and looping the samples, and would have been no less labor intensive, especially when the joints in Dilla's fingers would so often stiffen and swell.

"The one thing his mom will tell you is that he would go over the same track over and over again, making minute changes. I think [that's] why Chris was so pissed that Jeff was just going to get, like thrown out of the room if he brought an idea to edit the album over to him. Because Dilla was so meticulous about that," said Egon.

Whenever he selected the samples or where he was when he did so doesn't really matter; he still gravitated to songs with titles like, "You Just Can't Win," "I Can't Stand to See You Cry," "Sweet Misery," and the almost too on-the-nose, "When I Die." Much of his work from the 2005 batches, which turned up on Spacek's "Dollar," and posthumous releases like Mos Def's "History," or "Love" and "Won't Do" from *The Shining*, among others, strike a similarly restrained and thoughtful, if less chaotic, mood than what's heard on *Donuts*.

"I think a lot of the kind of, melancholy stuff, when I started hearing it was more or less when I knew that he was sick. So I think, in some ways, all of that kind of ties in together," said Waajeed.[7]

By the time he was making those beats, Dilla had been sick long enough, gone through enough treatments and hospital stays to have a sense of how his story might conclude, whether anyone else did or not. Kübler-Ross notes that, oftentimes, patients are the first to understand the severity of their conditions.

"[T]he outstanding fact, to my mind, is that [terminal patients] are all aware of the seriousness of their illness whether they are told or not. They do not always share this knowledge with their doctor or next of kin."[8]

Said B+, "Listen to *Donuts*. Do you really think the dude didn't know what was gonna happen to him? He fully knew what was gonna happen."[9]

"Like, his mom was in there like literally massaging his fingers, she tells that story and it's true. Like you know, and not only that, but she was taking like, not heaps of abuse, because it's her son, and he loved her and it was obvious, but you know the dude was going through some serious shit when he was making that final version of the record," said Egon.[10]

Any man who continues to make music until days before his death (Questlove once claimed the last beat Dilla ever made, a flip of Funkadelic's "America Eats Its Young," was made hours before he died),[11] who flies to Europe and performs from a wheelchair two months before his death, is Camus's ideal. Dilla's life was absurd in the extreme, but how he lived it despite that absurdity was heroic. If his illness was Sisyphus's rock, the descent was his music, the thing that made it bearable, even if it stared mortality in the face.

"When he passed, the shit just took on a whole new meaning … Like, was he really *that* nuts, to basically make a goodbye letter? That shit is like saying goodbye," said House Shoes.[12]

It's therefore not unreasonable to look at the album, to step into the sources used to make it and conclude that death and dying are present there: "[H]e really wasn't able to communicate. Which really makes *Donuts* that much creepier for me to hear because all of those [samples], I'm now certain beyond a shadow of a doubt, were actual messages from him," said Questlove.[13] It's only after repeated listens, when one gets "under the hood" of the tonal moods on the sampled records, that *Donuts* reveals it is not just sending messages about dying but about living as well.

The first stage of Kübler-Ross's model is denial; when faced with the news of oncoming death, patients initially cannot believe it, refuse to acknowledge that their time might be running short. That sense of denial doesn't appear often on the album, but that's not to say it's completely absent.

It's there in the album's proper opener, "Workinonit." The longest song on the album, and most traditionally structured, it offers listeners a false sense of security before the controlled chaos that erupts throughout the record's remaining 40 minutes. The beat's built around "The Worst Band in the World," a satirical take on stardom by British art-rock band 10cc. Dilla takes the loose jam of the original recording and turns it into the tightest rhythm section this side of the JB's, liberally inserting stabs of distorted guitar and choked sirens. There are vocal samples, mostly unintelligible save for the repeated mantra of "*play me, buy me, workin' on it*." The beat's a statement of intent, a declaration to people who might have forgotten about him in the years following Slum Village, Tribe, and Common that he was still here, still relevant, still working.

Yet, despite that confidence, there's a moment in the song's second movement where Dilla loops one last sample from the original's vocal. Coming at the end of the 10cc song, and playing on a motif of the band-as-product (in this case a vinyl record), the lyric on the original is *fade me*. When Dilla gets through with it, the sample seems to slur into something else entirely: *Save me*.

Denial is felt explicitly on "Dilla Says Go," where a sample of The Trammps assures the listener, "I'll get over it, baby." It's also there on beats that use well-worn samples, like the thundering drums from Mountain's "Long Red" on "Stepson of the Clapper" or the metallic grind of ESG's "UFO" on "Geek Down." These are not rare sources; most hip-hop fans would recognize them instantly even if they couldn't name them. But their use has a sense of finality, as though Dilla knew this would be his last pass, so he's going to prove just how dope he can make them. "Stepson" takes Mountain's live intro and turns it into a gospel breakdown, all clubbing drums, call and response vocals, and the audience applause looped into a soul clap. "Geek Down" takes ESG's guitars and plays with the gain, turning them nauseous, making them lurch and roll on top of a crushing drum break lifted from The Jimi Entley Sound, a one-off side project of Portishead members Geoff Barrow and Adrian Utley.[14]

These songs, and any time Dilla uses a staple of the genre, that abused shit he mentioned in the *Welcome 2 Detroit* liner notes, are challenges, the sort of nut-grabbing bravado that's been hip-hop's bread and butter from day one, the same challenge heard in every *Huh? What?* from Joeski Love. It's Dilla saying, "Could a dying man do this?!"

The second of the five stages manifests itself less overtly on *Donuts*, in that it permeates through some of the tracks, but it simmers beneath the surface most of the time. According to Kübler-Ross, "When the first stage of denial cannot be maintained any longer, it is replaced by feelings of anger, rage, envy, and resentment. The logical next question becomes, 'Why me?'"[15] This feeling of anger and resentment can be felt on the "skull-kicker" side of *Donuts'* twin moods. "The Twister (Huh, What)", "The Factory" and "Geek Down" all contain a sort of aggression in the way the drums are placed at the front of the mix; the kicks bludgeon, the snares crack like a slap to the face, and the hi-hats sizzle with treble. Anger also runs underneath the otherwise lovely song "Anti-American Graffiti" as Wolfman Jack barks about "a lot of sincere confusion about just what the doctor said," feeling overwhelmed ("too much to do!") and demanding to know, "who's going to take responsibility?"

But nowhere else on the album is anger and aggression felt more strongly than "Glazed." Compared to the other beats, "Glazed" is downright unpleasant, appearing as it does between the twin standouts "Time: The Donut of the Heart" and "Airworks." Dilla takes a one-bar horn break from Gene and Jerry's "You Just Can't Win," pushes up the high end and loops it *ad infinitum*. It's noisy, punishing, grueling, impossible to be anything besides what it is: What MC would ever try to rhyme over that? It's the only moment on the album where it feels as though Dilla is overtly getting in listeners' faces, challenging their endurance to see how much they can take, before rewarding them with the sublime "Airworks."

By the third stage, Kübler-Ross noticed that patients would start to accept the reality of their situation, but viewed it more as a problem to be solved, with an answer they could discover. As such, they start to bargain, try to cut deals, convinced there's something they can do to extend their lives: "The bargaining is really an attempt to postpone … and it includes an implicit promise that the patient will not ask for more if this one postponement is granted."[16]

Postponement. An attempt to squeeze more time out of a finite amount, to arrange for an event to take place at a later time. Postponement is at work in the greatest trick Dilla pulls on the entire album, checked by name on what might be its most moving track.

"Time: The Donut of the Heart" is a beautiful, wistful song, speeding up the intro to The Jacksons' "All I Do Is Think of You," and giving it the patented Dilla bounce; as strings wash over the background and the sound of a woman sighing in pleasure becomes a labored exhale of release. The song features the first appearance of Dilla's Dadaist vocal chopping, taking slices of Michael and his brothers so short they lose their meaning, and using them as tonal accents throughout the track. At the one-minute mark, Dilla slows the whole thing down (on the third beat no less), switching the hi-hat to eighth notes, halving the tempo of the guitar, and then speeds it up again on the one without missing a step. It's a prodigious display of drum programming for a producer who tapped out his drums by hand, but it's also his attempt to control time, to stretch it and pull it, to slow its progression through his music in ways he could not in his life.

Kübler-Ross also notes that much of the bargaining done during this stage is done via prayer. While Ma Dukes told the *Detroit Free Press* that Dilla became more spiritual in the last year of his life (often returning to the Book of Job), God isn't felt much throughout *Donuts*, with one exception: On "One Eleven," Smokey Robinson's sweet falsetto sings *Lord, have mercy*. It's not the centerpiece of the beat, that's the string melody from "A Legend in its Own Time" (another "King of the Beats" moment, perhaps), but it's there, and it's unobscured. It also doesn't appear to be taken from the record that serves as the basis for the rest of the beat, suggesting Dilla went out of his way to include it. For what it's worth, while the title most likely refers to nothing more than the length of the song, Chapter 1, Verse 11 of the Book of Job is the moment Satan dares God to test Job's faith by taking everything he has.

Bargaining is felt most concretely, though, on "Stop!" The song is one of the album's early high points, a return to a more solid song structure with a spacious introduction that gives listeners a chance to catch their breath after the whirlwind of music that starts the album. Dilla takes Dionne Warwick's warning to a trifling lover, chops it, rearranges it, and directs it back at the universe: *You better stop, and think about what you're doing, give a little back my way* … Dilla also makes good on the warning, pausing the music for one beat in the only outright moment of silence on the entire album, as if to say, "This is what happens if you go through with this."

"Stop!" actually went through the most changes during the album's many iterations. The version on the release is what was on the original beat tape, but sometime during the editing process, Dilla handed in a second version, a more straightforward loop with the silence removed. Jank asked for the older version back.

Individuals who enter the fourth stage, having begun to understand the reality of their situation and how little control they have over it, grow depressed and emotionally dark, grieving for their departure from the world. Many songs on *Donuts* "feel" sad ("Thunder," "The Factory," "Last Donut of the Night") but it's on "Walkinonit" that the emotions bubble to the surface. Over trilling strings, a refrain lifted from The Undisputed Truth's performance of the classic heartbreak song "Walk on By" repeats again and again with little variation: *Broken and blue, walking down the street, broken and blue*. The two lyrics come from entirely separate verses on the sample; they were put together deliberately. It's the rawest, least obfuscated moment on the album, almost confessional by comparison to everything else, making it all the more startling and powerful.

Finally, Kübler-Ross notes that if a patient has enough time to process their situation and make their way through the preceding stages, "He will have mourned the impending loss of so many meaningful people and places and he will contemplate his coming end with a certain degree of quiet expectation."[17]

Surprisingly, it's this stage of acceptance that becomes more noticeable after repeated listens, and is most present throughout. Many of the songs have a sense of closure, of settling affairs, and making peace: "Waves," another 10cc flip, takes the band's biker death ballad "Johnny Don't Do It," and morphs the title into a loop of *John—do—it*, likely a dedication to his younger brother John, now known as the MC Illa J; "People," "Don't Cry," and "U-Luv" seem explicit messages of comfort to the people he cares about. "Hi" is about reunion, of seeing someone again after a long time apart. In the original song, "Maybe" by Philadelphia soul trio The Three Degrees, the entire story started in that sample is told: The narrator speaks of leaving her man and regretting it, until she encounters him again at a bus stop and joins him for a drink, where she declares her love and begs for a second chance. Giving "Hi" an added air of mystery, Dilla offers no such resolution, he starts the narrative at the bus stop and ends it at the moment the speaker turns around; the listener has no idea what it is she sees when she does. It's a moment pregnant with unfulfilled expectation, and has a sense of hope; it's clear from the tone of the woman's voice she's pleased by what she finds behind her.

While it's likely unrelated to "Hi" but not insignificant, Ma Dukes told Ronnie Reese in *Wax Poetics* that during one stay in the ICU, Dilla wasn't fully coherent for two days and would ramble to himself, but she heard him talking to someone named "OD," murmuring "Okay, I'll wait on the bus, the white bus … okay, I won't get the red bus. Don't get the red bus." When she asked him about it later, Dilla told her he'd seen Wu-Tang MC Ol'Dirty Bastard, who died in 2004: "He explained that ODB told him not to catch the red bus—everyone that catches the red bus goes to hell. He was to wait for ODB and the white bus. Everyone that is true to the game, and true to their music, could have any ride that they wanted."

"Bye." reprises the tempo trick from "Time" but when it returns near the album's end, it has a different effect, faltering and regaining its balance like someone stumbling and regrouping his or her strength near the end of a long journey. It's a subdued track, as are most of the songs in the album's later moments, before exploding into one final burst of energy in "Welcome to the Show."

The last song on *Donuts* is typically the first *"A-ha!"* moment for listeners who begin to investigate the parts used to make the album. The song takes its sample from "When I Die" by 60s Canadian pop-rockers Motherlode and turns it into a hymn, looped outbursts of ecstatic joy. This isn't the muted optimism of a funeral, this is the raucous celebration of a New Orleans-style wake; Dilla's taking us to church. Amid the rapturous cries, a lyric begins to rise to the surface, out of context, but taken from a beautifully simple summation of what anyone might hope for when facing their end: *When I die, I hope to be the kind of man that you thought I would be.* The song then ends with the unexpected reprise of the Gary Davis-sampling "Donuts (Outro)" before cutting out and ending the album.

None of this is to say that Kübler-Ross's model is a checklist to be ticked off ("Done denying? Better get angry!"). It's not a linear or prescriptive model; she allowed that stages could overlap, and patients have also shown they can skip steps or double back and repeat. It's also not true to say that death pervades every song on the album; how dour an affair would that be? *Donuts* has humor (Frank Zappa's assurance that "you are going to dance, like you've never danced before!"; a tweak of the vocal that makes it seem as though "Lightworks" is encouraging everyone to "light up the spliffs"), and swagger ("The New"). Songs like "The Diff'rence" and "Two Can Win" are downright *happy*. Everyone ultimately faces their end alone, there's no prescription or rulebook for processing it, everyone faces it in their own way. Dilla faced it through music. As *Donuts* ends, one gets the sense he was coming to terms.

That is, if *Donuts* even *really* ends. Play the CD on "repeat all," and the end of "Welcome to the Show" feeds directly into the start of "Donuts (Outro)." The end is the beginning, the first is the last, and some things go on forever, like a circle. Like good music. Maybe like the human soul.

Dilla being Dilla, though, he couldn't let the ends of the album sync up perfectly: the transition between the two jerks and stutters just slightly as the album restarts. He always did love mistakes.

The New

As Dilla's final work, *Donuts* will always carry extra significance in the minds of many listeners. There's something about an artist's last work that seems to bring added resonance. According to the novelist John Updike, "[W]orks written late in a writer's life retain a fascination. They exist, as do last words, where life edges into death, and perhaps have something uncanny to tell us."[1]

If the presence of death and dying can be felt and heard throughout *Donuts*, if hidden messages are scattered throughout it, they don't explain why they're delivered in the ways in which they are. As the end point of a career that spanned over a decade and went through at least a quartet of distinct styles, it's hard to deny that *Donuts* is, at its most basic, *really weird*. To try and glean a sense of why that is, one must consider what it means for artists when they're faced with their expected or untimely end, and what that means for their art.

In 2006, the same year *Donuts* was released, the literary theorist Edward Said published *On Late Style*, a book that sought to explore why great artists and composers late in their lives (meaning near the end, not necessarily elderly) frequently produce work in one of two styles: A sort of creative final summation, the period at the end of the sentence as found in Shakespeare's *The Tempest*, or works that suggest not, "harmony and resolution but … intransigence, difficulty and unresolved contradiction."[2] With those moods at either end of the continuum, *Donuts* clearly falls along the latter.

Said draws heavily on the work of German philosopher Theodor Adorno, specifically what he had to say in a 1937 essay on the late works of Beethoven:

> For Adorno … those compositions that belong to [Beethoven's] third period … constitute … a moment when an artist who is fully in command of his medium nevertheless abandons communication with the established social order of which he is a part and achieves a contradictory, alienated relationship with it.[3]

Like Adorno's Beethoven, J Dilla was also an artist at the height of his powers, struck down by forces he could not control just as he ventured out into what would be the last phase of his career. The move to L.A., collaborations with Madlib, and an easy working relationship with Stones Throw seem to have given Dilla the freedom to move his art wherever he wanted. As a musician he had nothing left to lose, no limits or rules to concern himself with. And, if what Kübler-Ross suggests is true, he was acutely aware his window to do so was rapidly closing.

"I think mentally [moving] just kind of freed his mind, you know? It's a better way of life out here compared to where we were. I think it just freed him up to kind of think like, 'man, I can do whatever I want to do,'" said Frank Nitt.[4]

Since the publication of Said's book (written during his own late period as he battled leukemia and published posthumously), critics and scholars have been engaged in a sort of tug-of-war regarding the validity of his ideas. The most common criticism is that, considering each individual encounters death in his or her own way, one cannot shoehorn a universal theory of late style onto all circumstances, there are too many variables at play: Some artists have no idea death is imminent, some are aware of its possibility for years; some endure physical disabilities or diseases, some do not; some are elderly, some are taken tragically young. It's unreasonable to think that any theory of late style is applicable in all scenarios. Even the term itself falls under criticism: "[It] can't be a direct result of aging or death, because style is not a mortal creature, and works of art have no organic life to lose,"[5] writes Michael Wood in his introduction to Said.

But just because critics can't agree on a unified aesthetic for late style doesn't mean that late style, as a phenomenon, does not exist. One doesn't need to be a classical music scholar to notice the sweeping sonic and structural changes between Beethoven's "Moonlight Sonata" and the Ninth Symphony, first performed three years before his death and long after he started losing his hearing. Late style has been applied to Stravinsky, Strauss, and Schumann, and is equally applicable to J Dilla. Look at the adjectives frequently incorporated to describe what is considered "late style": Fragmentary, difficult, irascible, nostalgic, and introspective. *Donuts* can be legitimately described with an identical vocabulary. So where does Dilla's late style come from?

According to the scholar Joseph N. Straus, the one unifying characteristic among authors working in a late style is disability, not impending death, as death cannot typically be predicted accurately, but nonnormative bodily functions are something the artist endures every day: "[I]n the end *there may be nothing late about late style* in the sense of chronological age, the approach of life's end, or authorial or historical belatedness … late style may be less about anticipating death than living with disability, less about the future hypothetical than the present reality" (emphasis in the original).[6] Certainly, Dilla's present reality during the mixing of *Donuts* could be considered nonnormative, and was bound to have a psychological and physical impact on the music he made.

Ronnie Reese echoed Peanut Butter Wolf's comment to Egon before *Donuts* entered production, that a project of its sort was maybe the only thing Dilla *could* produce. "I think that it was the album that it was most feasible for him to make. You know, it's not like he can go to studios and master things or had access to a tremendous amount of equipment or gear when he was working on *Donuts*. So what he gave is the most he was able to give us at that time."

Like the Kübler-Ross model, late style theory is not intended to be a catch-all for all works by dying artists, and not every dying artist's work conforms to every aspect of late style: "It would be unlikely for any single work to exhibit all of these characteristics, but a late-style work would necessarily have most of them."[7] This is certainly true of *Donuts*.

Contrary to Said's argument regarding the late artist's contradictory relationship to the present, though, *Donuts* doesn't abandon the present social order as much as tilts its head at it in "What's up?" moment of acknowledgment, not just in its use of classic breaks and sounds but in specific response to the larger hip-hop landscape. "Dilla Says Go" takes the same sample source as "Hate It or Love It," a chart-topping single by L.A. rapper The Game released in early 2005, and makes something that sounds entirely different. More interestingly, "Stop!" uses the same Dionne Warwick sample as "Throwback," a 2004 song by the R&B singer Usher produced by Just Blaze. The song, like many contemporary R&B songs, features a rap break on the bridge, in this case provided by Jadakiss. In the opening moments of "Stop!" it's Jadakiss's voice that's manipulated to ask, "Is (death) real?" Is it a coincidence that Dilla took the same sample used on a song that came out the year before *Donuts* and even sampled the voice of that song's featured rapper? It's a question that can't be answered but it certainly seems too coincidental to be an accident. The choice may have been more intentional than anyone thought.

An online message board post attributed to Questlove, dated 2007 (its authorship is unverified, though it has a voice extremely similar to Questlove's writing from that time), alleges that the 2005 beats, including *Donuts*, were Dilla's "Kanye Batches" just as the process that led to the "Little Brother" beat came from the "Pete Rock Batches." They were the result of Dilla taking inspiration from what he was impressed by in hip-hop, and trying to put his own stamp on it.

"He told me that 'Spaceship' [from West's debut *The College Dropout*] fucked him up cause for the first time he never heard that interpretation of [Marvin Gaye's] 'distant lover' in his head when he heard 'distant lover'. kinda fucked him up a lil [*sic*]."[8] If the post is to be believed, for the first time in years, Dilla was actually taken aback by something he heard in hip-hop, a flip he never would have considered. So he tried not only to approximate the style popularized primarily by West and Just Blaze, he looked to master it, taking their soul-sampling approach, annihilating it, and reconstructing it into something wholly his own.

For all of these reasons, *Donuts* continues to exist as a late work in all its irascible, confrontational glory, continuing to challenge and irritate new listeners looking for insight into mortality with its occasionally impenetrable contradictions.

As the cultural critic Terry Teachout writes, "[M]ost of us want to know what to expect at the end of our own lives, and look to art to shed light on that dark encounter. But true artists, unlike the Hollywood kind, don't always tell us what we want to hear."[9]

Bye

February 9, 2013, at Detroit's Fillmore Theater, on one of the city's few remaining vibrant blocks along Woodward Avenue. The air carries a typically Midwestern chill, though the streets are mercifully clear of the snow brought in by a large system that rolled in off the Great Lakes and pummeled the city a week earlier. The lobby of the venue is like a bazaar, booths from local streetwear vendors, booksellers, and indie labels display their wares; Maurice Malone's Hip-Hop Shop must have felt like this 20 years ago.

A car pulls up to the front of the theater, crunching the curbside remains of pebble-flecked brown slush under its tires. A burly man in a crisply pressed black suit with a neatly trimmed beard and a wave in his hair steps out and opens the back door of the vehicle. He helps Ma Dukes exit the car and whisks her to the balcony entrance as security frisks ticketholders. She looks smaller in person, but it may be a visual trick caused by the sheer mass of the hulking man accompanying her: A cross between professional wrestler and Baptist preacher. He holds the door for her as she gives a quick wave to the smattering of people calling her name.

Mirroring his career in a way, this is only the second Dilla Day Detroit, despite annual parties being well established in places like New York, Los Angeles, and London for the last seven years.

"I wanted his name in lights in his own hometown ... we've got a young man doing incredible work that the whole world is admiring and [Detroiters] don't even know who he is," said Ma Dukes.[1] Tonight, her wish is granted: Along the marquee of the Fillmore, under the event's details, is a simple phrase, the plain truth behind every beat that touched the lives of the people waiting in line: *J Dilla has done the work*.

The crowd in attendance is a marketer's dream, a grab bag of demographics across race, gender, and age. They've come from Chicago, Cleveland, Toronto, and all over Michigan. They form a sea of Tigers caps as they walk into the concert hall. Some of the kids in the crowd must have been in pre-school when *Fan-tas-tic Vol. 1* began to circulate, when House Shoes was playing the freshest Dilla beats at St. Andrews. It's a testament to the timeless nature of Dilla's music. He's playing tonight, House Shoes. Along with Talib Kweli, DJ Spinna, Frank-n-Dank, and J. Rocc. Violinist and composer Miguel-Atwood Ferguson and a four-piece band play live arrangements of Dilla joints, written specifically for this night. Jazz saxophonist Allan Barnes makes an unannounced appearance, giving an impromptu solo rendition of "Think Twice," by his former teacher and bandmate, Donald Byrd, which Dilla covered in one of *Welcome 2 Detroit*'s more inspired and surprising moments. Lit by a lone spotlight on a darkened stage, Barnes's restrained performance in honor of Dilla and

Byrd, who passed the previous week, gives the crowd a chance to pause and reflect on the loss of two of Detroit's best. After Barnes finishes, a pair of men in their mid- to late 30s, dressed for the night in blazers, sweaters over collared shirts, and chains shining on their chests, each let out an impressed *Whooo* and give each other dap. "That is a talent I do not have," says one.

The evening seems as much an opportunity to celebrate Detroit as Dilla. The iconic Tigers' logo is projected large on the backdrop. The mayor of neighboring Highland Park says a few encouraging words about perseverance and hope, the director of a local gallery and hip-hop cultural center spins records between sets. When Ma Dukes hits the stage that night, she talks about ensuring the children of the city have choices and opportunities. Given Dilla's complicated relationship with his hometown, the place he repped until the day he died, smiling beneath the brim of his Tigers cap on the cover of *Donuts*, it's somewhat strange to watch the city try to reclaim him. Give people their flowers while they're here. Such talk is best saved for later. Tonight is for the music.

And there will be music. For nearly six hours the crowd is treated to classic hits and deep cuts, as well as notable songs Dilla sampled, a secret language shared among those in attendance. When Shoes drops "Open Your Eyes" by Bobby Caldwell, which Dilla flipped for Common's classic love song "The Light," a cheer goes up through the crowd. This song would be a piece of cruise ship schmaltz anywhere else, but tonight, in this room, in this crowd, it's a sacred text. Arms raised, fingers pointed to the sky, they sing in unison, they sing to strangers, they sing to friends, "*There are times, when you need someone, I will be by your side …*"

Five months later, the City of Detroit would file for bankruptcy, but tonight the spirit and will of its people feels unbreakable.

In the years since his passing, J Dilla's legacy has seen equal parts highs and lows. *The Shining*, estimated at 75 percent complete when Dilla died, was finished by Karriem Riggins at Ma Dukes's personal request, and released in August 2006. Other beat compilations have continued to trickle out over the years, notably the Pete Rock-curated *Jay Stay Paid* in 2009. Despite Dilla's assertion that the music on *Donuts* was too busy for an MC to handle, it hasn't stopped acts like The Roots, Common, or Busta Rhymes from rhyming over it. Ghostface Killah took the beat Dilla left for him by name ("One for Ghost") and released it as the appropriately comic yet longing "Whip You With a Strap" in 2006, a month after Dilla's passing. The song is a rare example of a *Donuts* beat being, not improved upon, but used to make something great in its own right.

In January 2013, Stones Throw rereleased *Donuts* as a box set of 45s, along with an extra disc of "Signs" and "Sniper Elite"/"Murder Goons," a pair of vocal tracks made during late 2005 (MF Doom rapping over "Anti-American Graffiti," and Ghostface Killah on "Geek Down," respectively). Pitchfork gave it a perfect score and named it "Best New Reissue."[2] Ma Dukes continues to work tirelessly, appearing at events around the world, giving interviews, and running the J Dilla Foundation, a non-profit that works to promote music education in the inner city. Dilla's brother Illa J released his first album

Yancey Boys in 2008, a collection of 14 songs made by his late brother. Bringing one story back around, he joined Slum Village in 2011.

Established MCs like Big Sean and Drake, or up-and-comers like Chance the Rapper and Joey Bada$$ continue to find inspiration in Dilla's music, dropping freestyles on mixtapes or name checking him in their verses. Jazz musicians such as pianist Robert Glasper and electronic artists like Flying Lotus compose and perform new arrangements of his work regularly, proving how versatile Dilla's music continues to be, how it works across genres and styles. In 2013 Kanye West told a documentary crew, as only Kanye West can, that Dilla's music, "felt like drugs. I mean, his music sounded like good pussy."[3]

Madlib rarely speaks about Dilla in interviews, when he does interviews at all. He said everything he cared to through two volumes of his *Beat Konducta* series in 2009, dedicated to the memory of his late friend and partner. Like *Donuts*, they're filled with their own mysteries and codes to unpack, sprinkled through a nonstop blend of funk and soul.

While his musical reputation continued to thrive after his passing, Dilla's estate was left in a shambles. As reported by Kelly Carter in a 2009 *VIBE* magazine article, Dilla's unpaid medical expenses and outstanding tax debts, combined with a breakdown in communication between his heirs and his executor, meant his family hadn't seen a dime from his work since his death. Things became so bizarrely litigious that Ma Dukes's initial attempts to start the foundation in her son's name were met with a cease and desist letter from his estate.

She later admitted her focus on taking care of her son may have been to the detriment of future financial security.

"He was trying to prepare me for over a year—so I'm not faultless. While I was there taking care of him for the two years, he always would be like, 'Okay, I want you to set up this, and I want you to do this. … [But] I didn't care because I thought he's gonna be alright. And even if I had to stay with him for the rest of his life, I knew he'd be alive and taking care of his business."[4]

In an effort to help her gain control of her son's estate, Egon obtained a lawyer for her, paid for with his own savings: "I wouldn't even have any money right now, if it wasn't [for] Jay Dee. So if I spent all of it, no matter how much it is, then at least I've done what I can with what he made possible for me," he said.

With Ma Dukes established as the primary executor of the estate, numerous projects once thought lost have started to trickle out. Frank-n-Dank's *48 Hours* finally saw proper release in 2013 after almost a decade of bootlegging, and at the time of this writing, Dilla's shelved vocal project is free from major label limbo and also scheduled for release. And there will likely be much more.

In the summer of 2012 a Detroit-area record store owner named Jeff Bubeck bought an abandoned storage unit that was filled with records, around 6,000, he told NPR: "Tons of seventies jazz, really a lot of off-the-wall, obscure stuff. There was a little bit of everything in there."[5] Impressed with enough of what he found, Bubeck bought the unit. Upon returning to it, he found a plastic tub tucked in the back, packed tightly with cassettes, and some junk mail addressed to a "James Yancey." Bubeck didn't think anything of it. Later, on a whim, he ran the name through an internet search, and learned he'd stumbled onto the mother lode of Dilla artifacts: Most if not all of his record collection, packed away after he left the D, and forgotten about once his mother left to join him in Los Angeles.

The second the news hit, social media exploded. "It was like instant backlash," said Bubeck. "'What business does he have selling Jay's stuff?' That's what it was. 'Who the fuck are you?'"[6] However, of greater interest was the knowledge that Bubeck had ended up with stacks of beat tapes that had never seen the light of day, even among Dilla completists who scoured the internet over the years searching for leaked batches. Though tempted briefly to sell them to the highest bidder, and threatened by an unnamed record company over their ownership, Bubeck, having learned the condition of Dilla's estate, ultimately decided to return them to Ma Dukes.

"I just felt … I'll be damned if I'm giving it to any record company. In the moment, I was just trying to do the right thing." Bubeck put a call in to Ma Dukes, took her to the storage unit and gave her the tapes. "It was her son's stuff, you know? I told her 'take it with you, it's yours.' It felt really good that she had it again."[7]

Ma Dukes was floored when she discovered the tapes not only contained beats, but rough song sketches and freestyles. "I didn't expect to hear his voice in any of the music … he's not sick, he's not suffering and he's just alive." Ma Dukes estimated the tapes contain hundreds of beats, enough to keep new Dilla material coming out for years. The first batch dropped in 2013, titled *The*

Lost Scrolls. For a woman who had lost so much in the struggle to preserve her son's legacy and music, she'd finally regained something precious.

"Dilla was my backbone, my support … when he left, I was standing alone. I never mourned normally, not knowing whether to be angry or to cry, I couldn't cry, I hadn't shed a tear … I was in denial of everything, I just had this void … [the tapes] brought back what Dilla had said to me in California. He was in the wheelchair, he grabbed my [hands] and he said, 'I want to thank you for all that you have done, and I want you to know, you're going to be all right, I promise you. You're gonna be all right.'"[8]

And for the first time, a mother cried for her son. Another circle completes.

Endnotes

Chapter One

1 Daniel J. Wallace, *The Lupus Book*, 5th edn (Oxford: Oxford University Press, 2013), 5.
2 Anslem Samuel, "J Dilla, The Lost Interview, Circa 2004," *XXL.com*, February 10, 2010, http://www.xxlmag.com/news/2010/02/j-dilla-the-lost-interview-circa-2004/3/
3 Kelly Carter, "Jay Dee's Last Days," *Detroit Free Press*, February 23, 2006, http://www.freep.com/article/20061127/ENT04/111270003/
4 "J Dilla Still Shining (Part 1 of 4)," YouTube Video, 8:30, posted by Bryan "B.Kyle" Atkins, February 11, 2011, http://www.youtube.com/watch?v=wMEWWKg0pz8
5 "Stussy—J Dilla Documentary Part 3 of 3," YouTube Video, 11:19, posted by "StussyVideo," May 25, 2011, http://www.youtube.com/watch?v=mOvYv79Lb6Q
6 Alvin Blanco, "J Dilla: Still Lives Through," *Scratch Magazine*, May/June 2006, http://thediggersunion.com/enjoy-and-be-educated/j-dilla-still-lives-through-scratch-magazine-mayjune-2006/

Chapter Two

1 Simon Trask, “Future Shock,” *Music Technology*, December 1988, http://www.mobeus.org/archives/juanatkins/
2 “Jeff Mills in 1997, old school, underground mixing + interview. Pt1,” YouTube video, 8:50, posted by “chvaxy,” September 13, 2011, https://www.youtube.com/watch?v=_A2CwGBDlLE
3 *Billboard*, “MC Breed,” http://www.billboard.com/artist/276847/mc-breed/biography
4 Carleton S. Gholz, “Welcome to tha D: Making and Remaking Hip Hop Culture in Post-Motown Detroit,” *Hip-Hop in America: A Regional Guide*, ed. Mickey Hess (Santa Barbara, CA: Greenwood Press, 2010), 397.

Chapter Three

1 Ronnie Reese, “Biography,” http://www.j-dilla.com/biography/
2 “KillerBoomBoxTV: A Conversation With Ma Dukes Pt. 1,” YouTube video, 13:19, posted by “KillerBoomBoxTV,” February 23, 2012, http://www.youtube.com/watch?v=R6pB2qvZNjY
3 Ronnie Reese, “Son of Detroit: Jay Dee Remembered,” *Wax Poetics*, June/July 2006, 99–110.
4 “KillerBoomBoxTV: A Conversation With Ma Dukes Pt. 1.”
5 *Ibid.*
6 Reese, “Biography.”

7 "Waajeed, DJ Spinna, Raydar Ellis discussing J Dilla at BEI, Part of BHF10 Week," YouTube video, 8:23, posted by "justhunte," July 13, 2010, http://www.youtube.com/watch?v=fugDzBQ0fuo
8 "J Dilla's Vinyl Collection—Crate Diggers," YouTube video, 26:44, posted by "fuse," March 20, 2013, http://www.youtube.com/watch?v=XL3ENrZwjmw
9 Reese, "Son of Detroit," 102.
10 Blanco, *Scratch Magazine*.
11 "KillerBoomBoxTV: A Conversation With Ma Dukes Pt. 1."
12 Dean Van Nguyen, "Kindred Soul," *Wax Poetics*, Issue 55, Summer 2013, 30.
13 Van Nguyen, "Kindred Soul," 32.
14 Reese, "Son of Detroit," 101.
15 Van Nguyen, "Kindred Soul," 32.
16 Marisa Aveling, "Detroit Lion," *Wax Poetics*, Issue 55, Summer 2013, 36–41.
17 Reese, "Biography."
18 Van Nguyen, "Kindred Soul," 32.
19 "Bling47 Breaks—Dilla Edition: Get This Money—DJ Spinna," YouTube video, 1:45, posted by "Bling47music," May 8, 2012, http://www.youtube.com/watch?v=p1ytpeDMKAU
20 The successor to *The Scene*, which took over the 6:00 p.m. timeslot on WGPR in 1988.
21 Hobey Eclin, "Dial 313 for the 411 on Hip-Hop," *Metro Times*, October 2–8, 1996, 21.
22 "Bling47 Dilla Breaks Edition: DJ Amir—Love," YouTube video, 2:28, posted by "Bling47music," February 15, 2012, http://www.youtube.com/watch?v=39HVVG02Lvo

23 Van Nguyen, "Kindred Soul," 30.
24 "Lecture: Q-Tip (New York, 2013)," online video, 2:05:53, posted by "Red Bull Music Academy," June 1, 2013, http://vimeo.com/67440689
25 Red Bull Music Academy, "Lecture: Q-Tip (New York, 2013)," http://www.redbullmusicacademy.com/lectures/q-tip
26 Referring to the level of quantization on Dilla's beats. Quantization refers to a process of automatically correcting improper drum timing by "rounding" the note to the nearest beat. Many samplers articulate this setting as a "swing percentage," to denote how rigid or loose the rounding is: Too much and the beat can sound artificial and mechanical, not enough and it can sound sloppy and off-time.
27 Red Bull Music Academy, "Lecture: Q-Tip" (New York, 2013).
28 *Ibid*.

Chapter Four

1 Don Hogan, "The J Dilla Interview," *RIME*, Issue 8, 2003, http://culturekingmedia.com/2010/02/07/j-dilla-interviewed-by-moonsatellite-for-rime-magazine-feature/
2 Jeff "Chairman" Mao, "Behind the Boards: The Legacy of Marley Marl," *Ego Trip*, Issue 12, http://www.egotripland.com/marley-marl-interview-ego-trip-magazine/
3 "Introducing Marley Marl!," YouTube video, 10:00, posted by "Diggiti," July 13, 2007, http://www.youtube.com/watch?v=vof_jmhBSU8

4 Bryan Coleman, *Check the Technique: Liner Notes for Hip-Hop Junkies* (New York: Villard Books, 2007), 250.
5 *Ibid.*, 305.
6 *Ibid.*, 307.
7 Fullerton, Jason, "J Dilla," *Attack and Rebuild*, March 2013, http://issuu.com/attackrebuild/docs/attackandrebuild-issue1#download
8 "J Dilla Still Shining (Part 2 of 4)," YouTube Video, 8:30, posted by Bryan "B.Kyle" Atkins, February 11, 2011, http://www.youtube.com/watch?v=eCMkaJtYtPY
9 Christopher R. Weingarten, "Pete Rock Slams Lupe Fiasco for Crappy 'T.R.O.Y.' Bite," *SPIN*, May 22, 2012, http://www.spin.com/articles/pete-rock-slams-lupe-fiasco-crappy-troy-bite/
10 A 2011 interview between the then 20-year-old Odd Future leader Tyler the Creator and Canadian weirdo Nardwuar saw Tyler wax rhapsodic when presented with records by jazz musicians Alan Tew and Roy Ayers.
11 Joseph G. Schloss, *Making Beats: The Art of Sample-Based Hip-Hop* (Middletown, OH: Wesleyan University Press, 2004), 122.
12 "Bling47 Dilla Breaks Edition: House Shoes—In the Streets," YouTube video, 3:01, posted by "Bling47music," October 1, 2012, http://www.youtube.com/watch?v=KN_07KaW2t8
13 Bootie Brown, Interview, *Jusayin Radio*, August 16, 2012.
14 James Yancey, liner notes to *Welcome 2 Detroit*, BBE, BBE BG CD 001, CD, 2001.

15 Late Night with Jimmy Fallon, "Questlove Explains "Little Brother's Beat," Hulu video, January 3, 2012, http://www.hulu.com/watch/315258
16 "J Dilla Still Shining (Part 2 of 4)," YouTube video, 8:30, posted by Bryan "B.Kyle" Atkins, February 11, 2011, http://www.youtube.com/watch?v=eCMkaJtYtPY

Chapter Five

1 "Stussy—J Dilla Documentary Part 3 of 3."
2 *Ibid.*
3 Interview via instant message, December 4, 2012.

Chapter Six

1 "Stussy—J Dilla Documentary Part 3 of 3."
2 James Yancey, interview by Gilles Peterson, *Gilles Peterson's World Wide*, BBC Radio 1, February 15, 2001, https://soundcloud.com/92bpm/jay-dee-w-gilles-petersons
3 Hogan, "The J Dilla Interview," http://culturekingmedia.com/2010/02/07/j-dilla-interviewed-by-moonsatellite-for-rime-magazine-feature/
4 Marley and Pete Rock both produced later entries of the series.
5 Anslem Samuel, "J Dilla, The Lost Interview [circa 2004]. *XXL*, February 10, 2010, http://www.xxlmag.com/news/2010/02/j-dilla-the-lost-interview-circa-2004/

6 Dean Van Nguyen, "Kindred Soul," *Wax Poetics*, Issue 55, Summer 2013, 32.
7 Peterson, *Gilles Peterson's World Wide*.
8 "J Dilla Still Shining (Part 2 of 4)."
9 Reese, "Biography."
10 Aadel Haleem, "Jay Dee Exclusive," *Urbandetour.com*, November 27, 2003, http://www.illmuzik.com/forums/threads/j-dilla-interview.3328/
11 Reese, "Biography."
12 Ahmir Thompson, "Questlove ?uestlove's Top 10 Life-Shaping Musical Moments (OG Version)," *Okayplayer.com*, October 27, 2011, http://www.okayplayer.com/stories/uestloves-top-10-life-shaping-musical-moments-og-version.html/10
13 Reese, "Son of Detroit," 107.
14 Adam Fleischer, "Questlove on Why J Dilla Was the Best Rap Producer of All Time," XXL, last modified February 11, 2012, http://www.xxlmag.com/news/2012/02/questlove-on-why-dilla-was-the-best-rap-producer-of-all-time/
15 Blanco, *Scratch Magazine*.
16 Samuel, "J Dilla, The Lost Interview."
17 Jon Caramnica, "Slum Village—Fantastic Volume II," [*sic*], *SPIN*, June 2000, 158.
18 Jason Birchmeier, "Slum Village—Fantastic, Vol. 2," AllMusic Guide, June 13, 2000, http://www.allmusic.com/album/fantastic-vol-2-mw0000602592
19 "J Dilla Still Shining (Part 2 of 4)".
20 Ronnie Reese, liner notes to Ruff Draft, Stones Throw Records, STH2153, CD, 2007.

21 Haleem, "Jay Dee Exclusive."
22 "Inside Dilla's Studio," YouTube video, 5:30, posted by "AgentV," April 26, 2006, http://www.youtube.com/watch?v=_OxH8riGZl8
23 Martin Turenne, "High Fidelity," *URB*, Issue 114, http://www.stonesthrow.com/news/2004/03/high-fidelity
24 *Ibid.*
25 "Stussy—J Dilla Documentary Part 1 of 3."
26 "Stussy—J Dilla Documentary Part 3 of 3," video, 11:18, posted by "Stussy," February 25, 2010, http://vimeo.com/9733848
27 "Stussy—J Dilla Documentary Part 1 of 3."
28 "Stussy—J Dilla Documentary Part 2 of 3," video, 8:12, posted by "Stussy," February 27, 2010, http://vimeo.com/9788481
29 Rhapsody, "In Memoriam—J Dilla The Rhapsody Interview," November 2006, http://www.rhapsody.com/artist/j-dilla/album/in-memoriam-j-dilla-the-rhapsody-interview
30 Reese, "Ruff Draft Liner Notes."
31 The cell fragment responsible for blood clotting.
32 Common, *One Day It'll All Make Sense* (New York: Atria Books, 2011), 249.
33 "Stussy—J Dilla Documentary Part 2 of 3."
34 Rodrigo Bascuñán, Luke Fox, and Joe Galiwango, "Dilla: One of the Best Yet," *Pound*, March 2006, http://www.poundmag.com/bullsh-t/dilla-one-of-the-best-yet/
35 Haleem, "Jay Dee Exclusive."
36 "Stussy—J Dilla Documentary Part 2 of 3."

37 "Houseshoes—From Detroit to L.A.," YouTube video, 10:09, posted by "ab0181," May 24, 2012, http://www.youtube.com/watch?v=fJckmxSlcRY
38 Stussy, "J Dilla Documentary Part 2 of 3."
39 Andre Torres, "Astral Traveler," *Wax Poetics*, Issue 56, Fall 2013, 56.
40 Reese, "Son of Detroit," 109.
41 *Ibid.*
42 "J Dilla's Vinyl Collection—Crate Diggers."

Chapter Seven

1 "Bling47 Dilla Breaks Edition: Rich Medina—History," YouTube video, 2:52, posted by "Bling47music," August 12, 2012, http://www.youtube.com/watch?v=V5s4OWinwzw
2 "J Dilla's Vinyl Collection—Crate Diggers."
3 "Stussy—J Dilla Documentary Part 3 of 3."
4 "Bling47 Dilla Breaks Edition: House Shoes—Ruff Draft Intro," YouTube video, 4:01, posted by "Bling47music," October 21, 2012, http://www.youtube.com/watch?v=f7FPV0qVF_8
5 "J Dilla's Vinyl Collection—Crate Diggers."
6 Interview via instant message, December 4, 2012.
7 Phone interview, January 18, 2013.
8 Interview via instant message, December 4, 2012.
9 Interview via instant message, December 4, 2012.
10 Carter, "Jay Dee's Last Days."
11 Ego Trip, "The Stories Behind 6 Iconic J Dilla Images with Photographer Brian B+ Cross," last modified February 9, 2013, http://www.egotripland.com/gallery/j-dilla-brian-cross-photos/23600/

12 For more on this see Andrew Gura "set wrap," last modified October 23, 2008, http://www.flickr.com/photos/trype_williamz/2966729377/
13 "Ruff Draft Interviews Part 4," YouTube video, 3:12, posted by "stonesthrow," March 28, 2007, http://www.youtube.com/watch?v=j7lbBS0f86c
14 "J Dilla Still Shining (Part 4 of 4)," YouTube video, 10:35, posted by Bryan "B.Kyle" Atkins, February 11, 2011, http://www.youtube.com/watch?v=hzx_-sEd3v0
15 Interview via instant message, December 4, 2012.
16 Thompson, ?uestlove's Top 10 Life-Shaping Musical Moments, 226.
17 Carter, "Jay Dee's Last Days."

Chapter Eight

1 Ahmir "Questlove" Thompson, *Mo' Meta Blues* (New York: Grand Central Publishing, 2013), 230.
2 Blanco, *Scratch Magazine*.

Chapter Nine

1 Ivan Tolstoy, *The Death of Ivan Ilych and Other Stories*, translated by Richard Pevear and Larissa Volokhonsky (New York: Knopf, 2009), 107.
2 Gordon Marino, "Introduction," *Basic Writings of Existentialism*, ed. Gordon Marino (New York: The Modern Library, 2004), xiv.
3 Albert Camus, *The Myth of Sisyphus*, translated by Justin Long (London: Penguin, 2005), 2.

4 *Ibid.*, 117.
5 Todd May, *Death* (Stocksfield: Acumen Publishing, 2009), 106.
6 Elisabeth Kübler-Ross, *On Death and Dying* (New York: Scribner, 1969), 22.
7 "Bling47 Dilla Breaks Edition: Rich Medina—History."
8 Kübler-Ross, *On Death*, 263.
9 "Stussy—J Dilla Documentary Part 3 of 3."
10 Phone interview, January 18, 2013.
11 Ryan Dombal, "5-10-15-20: ?uestlove," *Pitchfork*, last modified June 24, 2010, http://pitchfork.com/features/5-10-15-20/8474-5-10-15-20-uestlove/
12 "Stussy—J Dilla Documentary Part 3 of 3."
13 Fleischer, "Questlove on Why J Dilla Was the Best Rap Producer."
14 The break comes from the b-side of the project's only release, a cover of The Incredible Bongo Band's "Apache," one of the foundational breaks of hip-hop, and perhaps what drew Dilla to pick up the record in the first place.
15 Kübler-Ross, *On Death*, 63.
16 *Ibid.*, 97.
17 *Ibid.*, 124.

Chapter Ten

1 John Updike, "Late Works," *The New Yorker*, August 7, 2006, http://www.newyorker.com/archive/2006/08/07/060807crat_atlarge
2 Edward W. Said, *On Late Style: Music and Literature Against the Grain* (New York: Vintage, 2006), 7.

3 *Ibid.*, 8.
4 "Stussy—J Dilla Documentary 2 of 3."
5 Michael Wood, "Introduction," *On Late Style: Music and Literature Against the Grain* by Edward W. Said (New York: Vintage, 2006), xiii.
6 Straus, Joseph N., "Disability and 'Late Style' in Music," *The Journal of Musicology*, Vol. 25, No. 1 (Winter 2008), 6.
7 *Ibid.*, 11.
8 "Questlove on Dilla's Inspirations," Stones Throw Message Board, http://webcache.googleusercontent.com/search?q=cache:9VrxiWumegsJ:www.stonesthrow.com/messageboard/index.php%253Fshowtopic%253D4357+&cd=1&hl=en&ct=clnk&gl=ca
9 Terry Teachout, "Facing the Final Curtain," *The Wall Street Journal*, September 18, 2009, http://online.wsj.com/article/SB10001424052970204518504574418790035029918.html

Chapter Eleven

1 "Dilla Day Detroit—Talib Kweli, DJ Spinna, House Shoes & J. Rocc," YouTube video, 4:50, posted by "fuse," February 19, 2013, http://www.youtube.com/watch?v=tB5_TN4q80M
2 Nate Patrin, "J Dilla—Donuts (45 Box Set)," last modified January 16, 2013, http://pitchfork.com/reviews/albums/17510-donuts-45-box-set/
3 "Kanye West Talks Dilla, God & Pornography," Okayplayer, last modified June 25, 2013, http://www.okayplayer.com/news/

kanye-west-dilla-god-pornography-w-magazine.html

4 Kelly L. Carter, "Interview: Ma Dukes Speaks On Dilla's Legacy—And What Really Happened With His Estate," *Complex*, February 9, 2012, http://www.complexmag.ca/music/2012/02/interview-ma-dukes-speaks-on-dillas-legacy-and-what-really-happened-with-his-estate

5 National Public Radio, "J Dilla's Lost Scrolls," *Snap Judgment*, July 17, 2013, archived at https://soundcloud.com/snapjudgment/j-dillas-lost-scrolls?in=snapjudgment/sets/the-reunion

6 *Ibid.*

7 *Ibid.*

8 *Ibid.*

Works Cited

Print

Adorno, Theodor, "Late Style in Beethoven," *Essays on Music*, ed. Richard Leppert, translated by Susan H. Gillespe (Berkeley, CA: University of California Press, 2002).

Aveling, Marisa, "Detroit Lion," *Wax Poetics*, Issue 55, Summer 2013, 36–41.

Blanco, Alvin, "J Dilla: Still Lives Through," *Scratch Magazine*, May/June 2006.

Camus, Albert, *The Myth of Sisyphus*, translated by Justin Long (London: Penguin, 2005).

Caramanica, Jon, "Slum Village—Fantastic Volume II," [*sic*], *SPIN*, June 2000, 158.

Carter, Kelly Louise, "Dollars to Donuts," *VIBE*, February 2009, http://www.freep.com/article/20061127/ENT04/111270003/

Coleman, Bryan, *Check the Technique: Liner Notes for Hip-Hop Junkies* (New York: Villard Books, 2007).

Common, *One Day It'll All Make Sense* (New York: Atria Books, 2011).

Eclin, Hobey, "Dial 313 for the 411 on Hip-Hop," *Metro Times*, October 2–8, 1996.

Gholz, Carleton S., "Welcome to tha D: Making and Remaking Hip Hop Culture in Post-Motown Detroit," *Hip-Hop in*

America: A Regional Guide, ed. Mickey Hess (Santa Barbara, CA: Greenwood Press, 2010), 397–428.

Jank, Jeff, "Instrumental album from icon hip-hop producer," press release, 2006.

Kübler-Ross, Elisabeth, *On Death and Dying* (New York: Scribner, 1969).

Marino, Gordon, "Introduction," *Basic Writings of Existentialism*, ed. Gordon Marino (New York: The Modern Library, 2004).

May, Todd, *Death* (Stocksfield: Acumen Publishing, 2009).

Reese, Ronnie, "Son of Detroit: Jay Dee Remembered," *Wax Poetics*, June/July 2006, 98–110.

—Liner notes to *Ruff Draft*, Stones Throw STH2153, CD, 2007.

Said, Edward W., *On Late Style: Music and Literature Against the Grain* (New York: Vintage, 2006).

Schloss, Joseph G., *Making Beats: The Art of Sample-Based Hip-Hop* (Middletown, OH: Wesleyan University Press, 2004).

Straus, Joseph N. "Disability and 'Late Style' in Music," *The Journal of Musicology*, Vol. 25, No. 1 (Winter 2008), 3–45.

Thompson, Ahmir, "Questlove," *Mo' Meta Blues* (New York: Grand Central Publishing, 2013).

Tolstoy, Ivan, *The Death of Ivan Ilych and Other Stories*, translated by Richard Pevear and Larissa Volokhonsky (New York: Knopf, 2009).

Torres, Andre, "Astral Traveler," *Wax Poetics*, Issue 56, Fall 2013.

URB Magazine, "Jay Dee 1974 – 2006." April 3, 2006.

Wimsatt, W. K. and M. C. Beardsley, "The Intentional Fallacy," *The Sewanee Review*, Vol. 54, No. 3 (July–September 1946), 468–88

Wood, Michael, "Introduction," *On Late Style: Music and Literature Against the Grain*, Edward W. Said (New York: Vintage, 2006), xi–xix.

Yancey, James, Liner notes to *Welcome 2 Detroit*, BBE, BBE BG CD 001, CD, 2001.

Online

Bascuñán, Rodrigo, Luke Fox and Joe Galiwango, "Dilla: One of the Best Yet." *Pound*, March 2006. http://www.poundmag.com/bullsh-t/dilla-one-of-the-best-yet/ (last accessed June 5, 2013).

Billboard, "MC Breed—Biography," http://www.billboard.com/artist/276847/mc-breed/biography

Carter, Kelly L., "Jay Dee's Last Days," *Detroit Free Press*, February 25, 2006. http://www.freep.com/article/20061127/ENT04/111270003/Jay-Dee-s-last-days

—"Interview: Ma Dukes Speaks On Dilla's Legacy—And What Really Happened With His Estate," *Complex*, February 9, 2012. http://www.complexmag.ca/music/2012/02/interview-ma-dukes-speaks-on-dillas-legacy-and-what-really-happened-with-his-estate

Dombal, Ryan, "5-10-15-20: ?uestlove," *Pitchfork*, last modified June 24, 2010. http://pitchfork.com/features/5-10-15-20/8474-5-10-15-20-uestlove/

Ego Trip, "The Stories Behind 6 Iconic J Dilla Images with photographer Brian B+ Cross," last modified February 9, 2013. http://www.egotripland.com/gallery/j-dilla-brian-cross-photos/23600/

Fleischer, Adam, "Questlove on Why J Dilla Was the Best Rap Producer of All Time," *XXL*, last modified February 11, 2012. http://www.xxlmag.com/news/2012/02/questlove-on-why-dilla-was-the-best-rap-producer-of-all-time/

Fullerton, Jason, "J Dilla." *Attack and Rebuild*, March 2013. http://issuu.com/attackrebuild/docs/attackandrebuild-issue1#download

Gura, Andrew, "set wrap," last modified October 23, 2008. http://www.flickr.com/photos/trype_williamz/2966729377/

Haleem, Aadel, "Jay Dee Exclusive," *Urbandetour.com*, November 27, 2003. http://www.illmuzik.com/forums/threads/j-dilla-interview.3328/

Hogan, Don, "The J Dilla Interview," *RIME*, Issue 8, 2003. http://culturekingmedia.com/2010/02/07/j-dilla-interviewed-by-moonsatellite-for-rime-magazine-feature/

Mao, Jefferson, "Behind the Boards: The Legacy of Marley Marl," *Ego Trip*, Issue 12. http://www.egotripland.com/marley-marl-interview-ego-trip-magazine/

Reese, Ronnie, "Biography," http://realhiphop4ever.ucoz.com/blog/j_dilla_biography_written_by_ronnie_reese/2010-01-26-17

Samuel, Anslem, "J Dilla, The Lost Interview [circa 2004]," *XXL*, February 10, 2010. http://www.xxlmag.com/news/2010/02/j-dilla-the-lost-interview-circa-2004/

Teachout, Terry, "Facing the Final Curtain," *The Wall Street Journal*, September 18, 2009. http://online.wsj.com/article/SB10001424052970204518504574418790035029918.html

Thompson, Ahmir, "Questlove". "?uestlove's Top 10 Life-Shaping Musical Moments (OG Version)," *Okayplayer.com*, October 27, 2011. http://www.okayplayer.com/stories/uestloves-top-10-life-shaping-musical-moments-og-version.html/10

Trask, Simon, "Future Shock," *Music Technology*, December 1988. http://www.mobeus.org/archives/juanatkins/

Turenne, Martin, "High Fidelity," *URB*, March 2004. http://www.stonesthrow.com/news/2004/03/high-fidelity

Updike, John, "Late Works," *The New Yorker*, August 7, 2006. http://www.newyorker.com/archive/2006/08/07/060807crat_atlarge

Van Nguyen, Dean, "Kindred Soul," *Wax Poetics*, Issue 55, Summer 2013, 28–34.

Weingarten, Christopher R., "Pete Rock Slams Lupe Fiasco for Crappy 'T.R.O.Y.' Bite," *SPIN*, May 22, 2012. http://www.spin.com/articles/pete-rock-slams-lupe-fiasco-crappy-troy-bite/

Radio Interviews

BBC Radio 1, "Jay Dee Feature," *Gilles Peterson's Worldwide*, February 15, 2001. Archived at https://soundcloud.com/92bpm/jay-dee-w-gilles-petersons

Bootie Brown, "Interview," *Jusayin Radio*, August 16, 2012.

National Public Radio, "J Dilla's Lost Scrolls," *Snap Judgment*, July 17, 2013. Archived at https://soundcloud.com/snapjudgment/j-dillas-lost-scrolls?in=snapjudgment/sets/the-reunion

Rhapsody, "In Memoriam—J Dilla The Rhapsody Interview," November 2006. http://www.rhapsody.com/artist/j-dilla/album/in-memoriam-j-dilla-the-rhapsody-interview

Videos

"Bling47 Dilla Breaks Edition: Black Milk—Shake it Down," YouTube video, 2:52. Posted by "Bling47music," June 25, 2012. http://www.youtube.com/watch?v=rfnWGKWiiLk

"Bling47 Dilla Breaks Edition: DJ Amir—Love," YouTube video, 2:28. Posted by "Bling47music," February 15, 2012. http://www.youtube.com/watch?v=39HVVG02Lvo

"Bling47 Dilla Breaks Edition: DJ Spinna—Get This Money," YouTube video, 1:45. Posted by "Bling47music," May 8, 2012. http://www.youtube.com/watch?v=p1ytpeDMKAU

"Bling47 Dilla Breaks Edition: House Shoes—Ruff Draft Intro," YouTube video, 4:01. Posted by "Bling47music," October 21, 2012. http://www.youtube.com/watch?v=f7FPV0qVF_8

"Bling47 Dilla Breaks Edition: Rev Shines—Track 35," YouTube video, 1:59. Posted by "Bling47music," February 1, 2012. http://www.youtube.com/watch?v=5Q4QB6QSgFc

"Bling47 Dilla Breaks Edition: Rich Medina—History," YouTube video, 2:52. Posted by "Bling47music," August 12, 2012. http://www.youtube.com/watch?v=V5s4OWinwzw

"Detroit's Best Kept Secret (J Dilla)," YouTube video, 49:14. Posted by "Teaquest," August 1, 2009. http://www.youtube.com/watch?v=GcUYEXiDroE

"Dilla Day Detroit—Talib Kweli, DJ Spinna, House Shoes & J. Rocc," YouTube video, 4:50. Posted by "fuse," February 19, 2013. http://www.youtube.com/watch?v=tB5_TN4q80M

"DJ Spinna, Waajeed discuss J Dilla's Technique at BEI, part of BHF10," YouTube video, 8:17. Posted by "justhunte," July 13, 2010. http://www.youtube.com/watch?v=VM5J6AXv9_I

"Houseshoes—From Detroit to L.A.," YouTube video, 10:09. Posted by "ab0181," May 24, 2012. http://www.youtube.com/watch?v=fJckmxSlcRY

"Introducing Marley Marl!," YouTube video, 10:00. Posted by "Diggiti," July 13, 2007. http://www.youtube.com/watch?v=vof_jmhBSU8

"J Dilla Interviews Pt 1," YouTube video, 3:07. Posted by "stonesthrow," March 6, 2007. http://www.youtube.com/watch?v=oGZrjd6hMPc

"J Dilla Interviews Pt 2," YouTube video, 1:43. Posted by "stonesthrow," March 11, 2007. http://www.youtube.com/watch?v=eVoWm9qcxo0

"J Dilla Interviews Pt 3," YouTube video, 3:05. Posted by "stonesthrow," March 20, 2007. http://www.youtube.com/watch?v=xAlmingNBFg

"J Dilla Interviews Pt 4," YouTube video, 3:12. Posted by "stonesthrow," March 28, 2007. http://www.youtube.com/watch?v=j7lbBS0f86c

"J Dilla Interviews Pt 6," YouTube video, 3:07. Posted by "stonesthrow," April 16, 2007. http://www.youtube.com/watch?v=47olSdWCo0k

"J Dilla's Vinyl Collection—Crate Diggers," YouTube video, 26:44. Posted by "fuse," March 20, 2013. http://www.youtube.com/watch?v=XL3ENrZwjmw

"J Dilla Still Shining. (Part 1 of 4)," YouTube video, 8:30. Posted by Bryan "B.Kyle" Atkins, February 11, 2011. http://www.youtube.com/watch?v=wMEWWKg0pz8

"J Dilla Still Shining. (Part 2 of 4)" YouTube video, 8:30. Posted by Bryan "B.Kyle" Atkins, February 11, 2011. http://www.youtube.com/watch?v=eCMkaJtYtPY

"J Dilla Still Shining. (Part 4 of 4)," YouTube video, 10:35. Posted by Bryan "B.Kyle" Atkins, February 11, 2011. http://www.youtube.com/watch?v=hzx_-sEd3v0

"Jeff Mills in 1997, old school, underground mixing + interview. Pt1," YouTube video, 8:50. Posted by "chvaxy," September 13 2011. https://www.youtube.com/watch?v=_A2CwGBDlLE

"Kanye West Talks Dilla, God & Pornography," *Okayplayer*, last modified June 25, 2013. http://www.okayplayer.com/news/kanye-west-dilla-god-pornography-w-magazine.html

"KillerBoomBoxTV: A Conversation With Ma Dukes Pt. 1," YouTube video, 13:19. Posted by "KillerBoomBoxTV," February 23, 2012. http://www.youtube.com/watch?v=R6pB2qvZNjY

"Lecture: Q-Tip (New York, 2013)," online video, 2:05:53. Posted by "Red Bull Music Academy," June 1, 2013. http://vimeo.com/67440689

Patrin, Nate, "J Dilla—Donuts (45 Box Set)," last modified January 16, 2013. http://pitchfork.com/reviews/albums/17510-donuts-45-box-set/

"Questlove Explains "Little Brother's Beat," Hulu video, January 3, 2012. http://www.hulu.com/watch/315258

"Stussy—J Dilla Documentary Part 1 of 3," YouTube video, 8:50. Posted by "StussyVideo," May 25, 2011. http://www.youtube.com/watch?v=Op20Rab2pPg

"Stussy—J Dilla Documentary Part 2 of 3," YouTube video, 8:13. Posted by "StussyVideo," May 25, 2011. http://www.youtube.com/watch?v=DT77otLYAos

"Stussy—J Dilla Documentary Part 3 of 3," YouTube video, 11:19. Posted by "StussyVideo," May 25, 2011. http://www.youtube.com/watch?v=mOvYv79Lb6Q

"Waajeed, DJ Spinna, Raydar Ellis discussing J Dilla at BEI, Part of BHF10 Week," YouTube video, 8:23. Posted by "justhunte," July 13, 2010. http://www.youtube.com/watch?v=fugDzBQ0fuo

"Waajeed, Raydar Ellis, DJ Spinna discussing Dilla, the slum village at BEI," YouTube video, 9:14. Posted by "justhunte," July 13, 2010. http://www.youtube.com/watch?v=RX3scqKzsxU

Also available in the series

1. *Dusty in Memphis* by Warren Zanes
2. *Forever Changes* by Andrew Hultkrans
3. *Harvest* by Sam Inglis
4. *The Kinks Are the Village Green Preservation Society* by Andy Miller
5. *Meat Is Murder* by Joe Pernice
6. *The Piper at the Gates of Dawn* by John Cavanagh
7. *Abba Gold* by Elisabeth Vincentelli
8. *Electric Ladyland* by John Perry
9. *Unknown Pleasures* by Chris Ott
10. *Sign 'O' the Times* by Michaelangelo Matos
11. *The Velvet Underground and Nico* by Joe Harvard
12. *Let It Be* by Steve Matteo
13. *Live at the Apollo* by Douglas Wolk
14. *Aqualung* by Allan Moore
15. *OK Computer* by Dai Griffiths
16. *Let It Be* by Colin Meloy
17. *Led Zeppelin IV* by Erik Davis
18. *Exile on Main Sreet* by Bill Janovitz
19. *Pet Sounds* by Jim Fusilli
20. *Ramones* by Nicholas Rombes
21. *Armed Forces* by Franklin Bruno
22. *Murmur* by J. Niimi
23. *Grace* by Daphne Brooks
24. *Endtroducing . . .* by Eliot Wilder
25. *Kick Out the Jams* by Don McLeese
26. *Low* by Hugo Wilcken
27. *Born in the U.S.A.* by Geoffrey Himes
28. *Music from Big Pink* by John Niven
29. *In the Aeroplane Over the Sea* by Kim Cooper
30. *Paul's Boutique* by Dan LeRoy
31. *Doolittle* by Ben Sisario
32. *There's a Riot Goin' On* by Miles Marshall Lewis

33. *The Stone Roses* by Alex Green
34. *In Utero* by Gillian G. Gaar
35. *Highway 61 Revisited* by Mark Polizzotti
36. *Loveless* by Mike McGonigal
37. *The Who Sell Out* by John Dougan
38. *Bee Thousand* by Marc Woodworth
39. *Daydream Nation* by Matthew Stearns
40. *Court and Spark* by Sean Nelson
41. *Use Your Illusion Vols 1 and 2* by Eric Weisbard
42. *Songs in the Key of Life* by Zeth Lundy
43. *The Notorious Byrd Brothers* by Ric Menck
44. *Trout Mask Replica* by Kevin Courrier
45. *Double Nickels on the Dime* by Michael T. Fournier
46. *Aja* by Don Breithaupt
47. *People's Instinctive Travels and the Paths of Rhythm* by Shawn Taylor
48. *Rid of Me* by Kate Schatz
49. *Achtung Baby* by Stephen Catanzarite
50. *If You're Feeling Sinister* by Scott Plagenhoef
51. *Pink Moon* by Amanda Petrusich
52. *Let's Talk About Love* by Carl Wilson
53. *Swordfishtrombones* by David Smay
54. *20 Jazz Funk Greats* by Drew Daniel
55. *Horses* by Philip Shaw
56. *Master of Reality* by John Darnielle
57. *Reign in Blood* by D. X. Ferris
58. *Shoot Out the Lights* by Hayden Childs
59. *Gentlemen* by Bob Gendron
60. *Rum, Sodomy & the Lash* by Jeffery T. Roesgen
61. *The Gilded Palace of Sin* by Bob Proehl
62. *Pink Flag* by Wilson Neate
63. *XO* by Matthew LeMay
64. *Illmatic* by Matthew Gasteier
65. *Radio City* by Bruce Eaton
66. *One Step Beyond . . .* by Terry Edwards
67. *Another Green World* by Geeta Dayal
68. *Zaireeka* by Mark Richardson
69. *69 Love Songs* by L. D. Beghtol
70. *Facing Future* by Dan Kois
71. *It Takes a Nation of Millions to Hold Us Back* by Christopher R. Weingarten
72. *Wowee Zowee* by Bryan Charles
73. *Highway to Hell* by Joe Bonomo
74. *Song Cycle* by Richard Henderson
75. *Spiderland* by Scott Tennent
76. *Kid A* by Marvin Lin

78. *Pretty Hate Machine* by Daphne Carr
79. *Chocolate and Cheese* by Hank Shteamer
80. *American Recordings* by Tony Tost
81. *Some Girls* by Cyrus Patell
82. *You're Living All Over Me* by Nick Attfield
83. *Marquee Moon* by Bryan Waterman
84. *Amazing Grace* by Aaron Cohen
85. *Dummy* by R. J. Wheaton
86. *Fear of Music* by Jonathan Lethem
87. *Histoire de Melody Nelson* by Darran Anderson
88. *Flood* by S. Alexander Reed and Elizabeth Sandifer
89. *I Get Wet* by Phillip Crandall
90. *Selected Ambient Works Volume II* by Marc Weidenbaum
91. *Entertainment!* by Kevin J.H. Dettmar
92. *Blank Generation* by Pete Astor
93. *Donuts* by Jordan Ferguson
94. *Smile* by Luis Sanchez
95. *Definitely Maybe* by Alex Niven
96. *Exile in Guyville* by Gina Arnold
97. *My Beautiful Dark Twisted Fantasy* by Kirk Walker Graves
98. *The Grey Album* by Charles Fairchild
99. *()* by Ethan Hayden
100. *Dangerous* by Susan Fast
101. *Tago Mago* by Alan Warner
102. *Ode to Billie Joe* by Tara Murtha
103. *Live Through This* by Anwen Crawford
104. *Freedom of Choice* by Evie Nagy
105. *Fresh Fruit for Rotting Vegetables* by Michael Stewart Foley
106. *Super Mario Bros.* by Andrew Schartmann
107. *Beat Happening* by Bryan C. Parker
108. *Metallica* by David Masciotra
109. *A Live One* by Walter Holland
110. *Bitches Brew* by George Grella Jr.
111. *Parallel Lines* by Kembrew McLeod
112. *Workingman's Dead* by Buzz Poole
113. *Hangin' Tough* by Rebecca Wallwork
114. *Geto Boys* by Rolf Potts
115. *Dig Me Out* by Jovana Babovic
116. *Sound of Silver* by Ryan Leas
117. *Donny Hathaway Live* by Emily J. Lordi
118. *Psychocandy* by Paula Mejia
119. *The Modern Lovers* by Sean L. Maloney
120. *Soundtrack from Twin Peaks* by Clare Nina Norelli
121. *Colossal Youth* by Michael Blair and Joe Bucciero
122. *Bizarre Ride II the Pharcyde* by Andrew Barker

123. *The Suburbs* by Eric Eidelstein
124. *Workbook* by Walter Biggins and Daniel Couch
125. *Uptown Saturday Night* by Patrick Rivers and Will Fulton
126. *The Raincoats* by Jenn Pelly
127. *Homogenic* by Emily Mackay
128. *Okie from Muskogee* by Rachel Lee Rubin
129. *In on the Kill Taker* by Joe Gross
130. *24 Hour Revenge Therapy* by Ronen Givony
131. *Transformer* by Ezra Furman
132. *Drive-By Truckers' Southern Rock Opera* by Rien Fertel
133. *Siouxsie and the Banshees' Peepshow* by Samantha Bennett
134. *dc Talk's Jesus Freak* by Will Stockton and D. Gilson
135. *Tori Amos's Boys for Pele* by Amy Gentry
136. *Odetta's One Grain of Sand* by Matthew Frye Jacobson
137. *Manic Street Preachers' The Holy Bible* by David Evans
138. *The Shangri-Las' Golden Hits of the Shangri-Las* by Ada Wolin
139. *Tom Petty's Southern Accents* by Michael Washburn